MY NORTH EAST

BY ITS FAMOUS SONS AND DAUGHTERS

EDITED BY

ANNE GRAHAM AND MICHAEL HAMILTON

LANDSCAPE PHOTOGRAPHY BY GRAEME PEACOCK

DESIGN BY JEREMY HOPES

Published by Kingfisher Reach Communications Ltd
Little Acre
Witton Gilbert
Durham
DH7 6TL
www.my-northeast.co.uk

First published in 2013

All landscape photographs by Graeme Peacock of
www.graeme-peacock.com except where otherwise credited

ISBN 978-0-957689-70-1

Printed and bound in the United Kingdom by Elanders, North Tyneside, NE27 0QG
www.elanders.com

elanders
UNITED KINGDOM

CONTENTS

Acknowledgments

In so many ways and to so many people, Sir Bobby Robson was an inspiration.

When I spoke to him in 2008 about the launch of The Sir Bobby Robson Foundation he talked passionately about his aspirations for the charity and what he hoped it would achieve in the region. He wanted to make a difference in the very area where his own roots lay. History has shown that the Foundation has exceeded even Sir Bobby's hopes and dreams – and continues to do so.

Wherever he went in the world, the North East was always in his soul. He cared about the place and its people, and he would often reminisce about the County Durham village of Langley Park where he spent his childhood – and where I, too, grew up.

After his death in 2009, when I was talking about Sir Bobby to fellow North Easterners, it became clear that they also shared his fierce loyalty and deep affection for this unique part of the world.

And that's how the book was born. We've brought together for the first time in words and images what home means to many of the region's famous sons and daughters – including Sir Bobby.

So thank you, Bob, for the inspiration. I hope we've done you justice.

Anne Graham, co-editor

Many thanks to all the sons and daughters of the North East who are featured in this book, with special thanks for their help, advice and guidance to Ray Laidlaw and Ian La Frenais.

Thanks also to: the Sir Bobby Robson Foundation; Inpress, Newcastle; Beamish Museum; English Heritage; National Trust; ITV; BBC; Sky Sports; North News & Pictures; Mark Savage Photography; Newcastle United Football Club; Sunderland Association Football Club; Middlesbrough Football Club; Rex Features; the Sage Gateshead; ncjMedia Ltd; the Variety Club of Great Britain; Elanders, North Tyneside.

All profits from My North East will be donated to The Sir Bobby Robson Foundation (Newcastle upon Tyne Hospitals NHS Charity Reg. 1057213). Find out more about the Foundation's work at www.sirbobbyrobsonfoundation.org.uk

FOREWORD

WE LEFT THE NORTH EAST IN THE 1950s and travelled to wherever Bobby's job took him. The region was always in our hearts but we didn't know when – or if – we would return until the call came from Newcastle United.

So it was that, in 1999, we came back home. As Bobby said, it was the best thing we ever did and we picked up with family and friends as if we had never been away. Some things had certainly changed in many, many ways but we felt the fundamental friendliness of the people and the beauty of the towns, countryside and coastline was the same.

I think many of the personalities featured in this book have similar feelings. It's clear that the region has a strong pull for everyone, whether they live elsewhere, travel frequently for their work or have put down permanent roots.

I'm delighted that so many of the best-known sons and daughters of the region have been happy to share their love for the North East, especially their personal favourite places, some of which are famous, iconic views and others which are less familiar but particularly precious to them.

It is wonderful that the profits from this book will go to the Sir Bobby Robson Foundation, which we launched in 2008 and which has gone from strength to strength ever since. This book will play a small part in helping us keep up the good work.

LADY ELSIE ROBSON

DONNA AIR

actress and TV presenter

Her career started in the TV series Byker Grove, *then Donna became part of the pop act Crush. She later went on to be a TV presenter and she has continued acting on television and in films. She is also known for her extensive charity work and is a pioneer of organic food.*

I WAS ONLY TEN YEARS OLD when I joined the cast of *Byker Grove* – a great show for a girl born and bred in Newcastle. It was set in The Mitre, a fictional after-school club, and was actually filmed in Benwell in the west of the city, not Byker itself. It was my second home and I worked on the show for five or six years. It launched a lot of people's careers including Ant & Dec and Jill Halfpenny. With *Byker Grove* now gone, the region is missing a real stepping-stone for talented youngsters.

As it happened, I used to spend a lot of time in the real Byker where my grandparents lived. I'd stay with them a lot in those days and I used to go to youth clubs. There was always something to do.

There was none of that over-protective stuff going on in my family. My parents would just say: "If you want to do something, just get on with it, pet." So I did. I left home to be in the pop group Crush when I was only about 15. I moved to Windsor and lived with a chaperone for a while, and the group went off touring to America and south east Asia so it was an exciting time and I never moved back home.

I miss Newcastle, though, and I love coming back to visit and see the family – these days with my own daughter. We like to stay in Jesmond Dene where I used to go for long walks with my granddad, and I still enjoy walking round there. The place is so pretty and there are some lovely places to eat. That's something that I really notice when I come back now. There is so much more attention on fantastic local produce. I like to go to food markets and farm shops to see what's on offer, and the fish market in North Shields is terrific.

Another thing that gets better and better is the focus on the arts. People in the North East have always been receptive to anything to do with the arts, and you can see that not just in music and theatre but also in galleries like the Baltic which is really impressive.

Donna with Ant & Dec at a Byker Grove *reunion*

That's one of the reasons I love performing at the Sunday for Sammy shows which are staged every two years at Newcastle City Hall and which raise money to help local youngsters get on in the performing arts. It's a great project.

The important thing for me is to do work that I believe in and enjoy. I don't measure success by how many people see whatever I'm doing but on whether it's good quality. For me, when I'm acting for instance, it doesn't matter if it's in a play round the corner or in the West End or in my kitchen!

I'm most proud of the fact that, no matter what happens, I get up every day and work hard and try to do my best. I think part of that comes from my upbringing and the feistiness that's part of most people in the North East. There's a no-nonsense attitude but also a lot of heart and soul. There's a genuine warmth and charm – even if someone is telling you to shut your face!

Being from Newcastle makes it the star of the region for me. There's a great history there and an energy like no other place. It has a vigour, pace and excitement which drives people on and makes them determined. We don't tolerate any excuses.

@donnaair

"We like to stay in Jesmond Dene where I used to go for long walks with my granddad, and I still enjoy walking round there."

ALEXANDER ARMSTRONG

comedian, actor, presenter and author

Alexander Armstrong, half of BAFTA-winning comedy duo Armstrong and Miller, starred in Love Life, Life Begins, Mutual Friends *and* Hunderby. *He has hosted* Pointless, Alexander Armstrong's Big Ask, Epic Win *and* Have I Got News For You, *published* The 100 Most Pointless Things in the World *and* The 100 Most Pointless Arguments in The World *alongside Richard Osman, and performs in Alexander Armstrong and his Band.*

I WAS BORN in the Rothbury Cottage Hospital, delivered – like nearly all of my contemporaries in the area – by my father. We have a long history of medicine in our family. My grandfather Rex had been the doctor before Dad and if I'd chosen to be the next Rothbury doctor I'd have been the ninth generation of my family to practise medicine in the North East.

We lived a few miles down the river from Rothbury, near Pauperhaugh. Pauperhaugh calls itself a village which I think is stretching it as it consisted only of one farm, one post office in the front of the old smithy and a phone box for which old Mrs Carr the postmistress had cut a square of carpet and would put in a new vase of fresh flowers every week.

It would be hard to think of a more idyllic childhood; our nearest neighbours were a mile away, but we had everything we wanted, fishing on the Coquet a ten-minute walk away, perfect bike-riding country, woods to build dens in, a burn to swim in, and best of all every winter we got snowed in which meant the Christmas holidays went on much longer than expected.

We still have our cottage in Craster, famous for its kippers and about 20 miles away from Pauperhaugh. That was the scene of many happy holidays and is now very popular with our children who do exactly the same things we used to do. By day the tiny village thoroughfare would be crowded with people, snippets of whose conversations would drift into our open windows and then, magnificently, at 6pm they would all disappear and the village with its bobbing fishing boats and its beautiful pier would empty and feel like ours again.

There's nowhere like the North East – it retains a strong sense of its history without being self-conscious about it. As a family we wouldn't think of having a get-together that didn't involve singing songs: *The Blaydon Races*, *The Lambton Worm*, *Cushy Butterfield* and *Keep Yer Feet Still, Geordie Hinny* all get a regular airing and it's a point of honour to know the words to as many verses as possible. It's a hoary old cliché, but the people of the North East are the warmest-hearted people I've ever known.

My favourite place in the world is the Coquet Valley, from Hepple downstream to Thropton, Rothbury, and on to Brinkburn Priory where my Fenwick ancestors used to live. The view across the valley from Simonside is one I think of often and it always gives me solace.

The North East has a record like no other region for holding on to its people. The Armstrongs came originally from Liddesdale and Cumbria but settled around Rothbury in the 19th century. If I could find a way to make it work around my filming schedule we would move back to the North East in a heartbeat. We had a family holiday last summer in Northumberland and I hope it will become an annual fortnight so that our boys can learn all about a place where they have deep, deep roots.

"We still have our cottage in Craster, famous for its kippers and about 20 miles away from Pauperhaugh. That was the scene of many happy holidays and is now very popular with our children who do exactly the same things we used to do."

"My favourite place in the world is the Coquet Valley, from Hepple downstream to Thropton, Rothbury, and on to Brinkburn Priory where my Fenwick ancestors used to live. The view across the valley from Simonside is one I think of often and it always gives me solace."

PETER BEARDSLEY MBE

footballer and football coach

Peter Beardsley began his football career with Carlisle United in 1979 before spells with Newcastle United, Liverpool and Everton in an illustrious 20-year playing career. In 1987 he set a record transfer fee of £1.9 million and played for England 59 times between 1986 and 1996. He now works as Football Development Manager for Newcastle United.

I'M A CITY BOY and I still love coming home to Newcastle on the train if I've been away in London, and looking down the river to all the Tyne bridges. It's especially striking at night when it's all lit up. I feel like I'm home when I see the Tyne Bridge or if I'm driving back when I see the Angel of the North.

When you come into Newcastle you can see St James' Park from whatever direction you arrive. It completely dominates the city skyline. Every day I get a terrific view of Sir Bobby Robson's statue outside the ground. It's like he is still watching over us. And on match day when I walk past it I can't resist giving him a little wink.

I grew up in Longbenton in the mid-Sixties and there wasn't a lot of money around. My dad Sammy was a long-distance lorry driver and I really don't know how my mam Catherine coped bringing up me, my two older brothers George and Ronnie and younger sister Sandra. The first place we went on holiday was Crimdon Dene. I didn't even get on a plane until I was 21 and joined Vancouver Whitecaps from Carlisle. We would go down to Whitley Bay for day trips in the summer holidays on the bus. It was long before the Metro was built. I loved Whitley Bay. I was devastated when they got rid of the Spanish City, even though I was 40-odd at the time!

I'm as proud as punch to be from the North East. It's the greatest place on earth to live. Every day I drive past my old secondary school Longbenton High – it's now Longbenton Community College – and I go past the cemetery where my mam, dad and sister are. I drive past the football pitches where I learned my craft as a kid to arrive at work every day at Newcastle United's training ground in Darsley Park in Benton.

I have great memories of playing for Wallsend Boys' Club in the Sixties. It rightly had a great reputation as a finishing school for young footballers. There would be four or five top professional football scouts at every game. I owe a great debt to Peter Kirkley and Brian Watson who had faith in me and got me my big break at Carlisle thanks to Bob Moncur, the manager who took me on there at 16. He's an honorary Geordie in my eyes for winning the Fairs Cup for Newcastle as club skipper in 1969.

My first wage was £30 a week and I thought it was a fortune back then. I've never been motivated by money – I was just delighted to be playing professional football. But within six weeks I was in the first team and Bob doubled my wages and got me on a four-year contract. I lived with Bob and his wife Camille back then and I remember my first pre-match meal was steak and roast potatoes. We didn't have dieticians in those days – I used to eat three packets of chocolate buttons before a match. Happy days!

I'll never forget joining Newcastle as a player for the first time in September 1983. I was playing for Vancouver Whitecaps when I got a call from the manager Arthur Cox. He said: "I want you to play up front alongside Kevin Keegan." I was looking around for the camera because I thought it was a wind-up! He told me the deal was done with the Whitecaps and he knew what I got paid. I was on £400 a week but I took a pay cut – £100 a week – to play alongside Keegan.

Kevin was actually on the same shuttle flight to Newcastle from London as me on my first day back. I had flown in from Vancouver. I knew who he was.

Kevin Keegan with Peter Beardsley

Someone must have told him who I was. He came over and said: "It's great to have you on board, but I've never heard of you. I hope you are as good as Arthur says." From the first morning in training he called me Pedro and that nickname has stuck to this day. It's even on my car number plate.

Playing for England with Bobby Robson as the manager was a dream come true. On the morning of my third match against Russia in 1986 – I had played poorly against Egypt and Israel, to be fair – Bobby said to me in front of everyone: "This is your last chance."

I made a goal for Chris Waddle and we won 1-0. Straight after the game he told me I was going to the Mexico World Cup. He said: "Don't tell anybody." I only told my wife Sandra. That was unbelievable – it was three months away. He treated me like a king. In fact he was brilliant with all the North East lads in the England squad – myself, skipper Bryan Robson, Chris Waddle and Gazza. He always looked after us and made us feel extra special.

www.nufc.co.uk

"I feel like I'm home when I see the Tyne Bridge. It's especially striking at night when it's all lit up."

MARK BENTON

actor

Mark Benton has been on television and in theatre for more than 20 years and forged a career as a top character actor in dramas, including BBC TV's Waterloo Road *and* Early Doors, *and stage roles with the National Theatre and the Royal Shakespeare Company. He also starred in* Strictly Come Dancing *in 2013.*

I'M A SOFT SOUTHERNER NOW! I live in Hastings with my wife and three children but I try and get up to the North East as much as I can, certainly four or five times a year. I miss it and love coming home. I still support the 'Boro, of course, but I had to give up my season ticket because I just wasn't getting to many games because of work and family commitments. My sister Dawn is a dinner lady living in Redcar, and my brother Ian is an insurance man. I always try and stay with my dad Tommy when I come up home. He was a lorry driver but he's retired now and living a life of leisure. My family have always been a tremendous support including my mum Glynne, God bless her – she passed away in 2008. I guess they are proud of what I've achieved. I definitely get my sense of humour from my dad.

There are always a few teachers who are inspirational when you are growing up. I grew up in Grangetown and went to the old Sarah Metcalfe School. I remember Mr Brighton who was my form teacher and a lovely man, and my drama teacher Ann Tighe was great. Later there was Gordon Steel and Anne Atwood who I did youth theatre with. My uncle Michael Gunn is an actor and I think, initially when I was young, I wanted to be like him. I used to come home from school and he would be there with his tales. At school I did a few plays then I went to Billingham Technical College and I would do as many local productions as I could. Anything I could get my hands on.

It was always acting or music when I was growing up. I was always in bands. I tried to write stuff but the people who were in the band were actually really talented musicians and better singers than me too. First off

As teacher Chalky in the BBC TV drama Waterloo Road

we were a heavy metal band called Stallyon – the 'y' was very important in the spelling of course – and we then morphed into a pop funk band called Face Moods. We took the name from a poster on the music room wall because we couldn't think of one ourselves. It was a terrible name. We played a few gigs at school and on local radio but we split up before we got anywhere. The band included Paul Tilley the drummer, who is still making a living as a professional musician, gigging and teaching drums.

I tried for drama school at 18 but didn't get in then tried again at 20 and got into RADA. I found RADA pretty down-to-earth really. My year in particular was a real mix of different people with different backgrounds so it was great. I had a brilliant time. It was totally unlike I thought it would be. There were some public school types but it certainly wasn't all stuck-up posh people. It was wonderful training. My family and friends have got used to it over the years. But for someone from my background to go away and become a successful actor, it took some getting used to for them – and at the same time to realise I was still the same me. But they are supportive and try and catch the things that I am in, and they are usually complimentary about what I do!

I love the view from Eston Nab. It's a rocky outcrop like a big chimney on top of Eston Hills and from the top you can see over all of Teesside. There's an Iron Age hill fort there but locals like it because it's a brilliant viewpoint. We used to go up there when we were kids, sit on top of the world and enjoy looking down. You can see way over to Redcar and Stockton.

"I love the view from Eston Nab. It's a rocky outcrop like a big chimney on top of Eston Hills and from the top you can see over all of Teesside. We used to go up there when we were kids, sit on top of the world and enjoy looking down."

TONY BLAIR

former Prime Minister

Tony Blair was Prime Minister of Great Britain and Northern Ireland from 1997-2007, and served as the Member of Parliament for Sedgefield from 1983-2007. Since leaving office he has established three charities and also works to promote peace and prosperity in the Middle East in his role as Quartet Representative. He is married to Cherie, and they have four children.

THE NORTH EAST WILL ALWAYS BE HOME, no matter how long I spend away. There's nothing quite like the view from the train as you pull in to Durham to remind you that you're back where you belong.

I owe a huge amount to this part of the country. I spent a happy childhood here. I passed my driving test on Durham's streets. This region gave me my love for Newcastle United although, as I'm sure the great Sir Bobby Robson witnessed when he coached me at an event back in 2005, my talent rests firmly in the spectator stands.

And the North East is where my political career began. Without the support of people from this part of the country, getting to Downing Street would have been impossible.

I was born across the border in Edinburgh in 1953. After a short detour via Adelaide, Australia, my family settled in Durham – close to the university where Dad was a lecturer.

Durham was a wonderful place to grow up. Familiarity can often blind you to the beauty of a place, but I have never lost my appreciation of what makes it so special. And it's clear from the thousands of tourists who flock to take in the cobbled streets of the old centre, the stunning Norman architecture of the cathedral, and the history of the university, that I'm not alone in my love for this place.

But it's not just the city of Durham that draws you in. The beauty of the county to which it gives its name cannot be rivalled. Stunning areas like Teesdale and Weardale, and the lovely village of St John's Chapel where I spent many happy days.

Derwent Reservoir from Blanchland looking over Weardale and Northumberland

"The beauty of the county cannot be rivalled, with stunning areas like Teesdale and Weardale."
High Force – one of England's most dramatic waterfalls

"Durham was a wonderful place to grow up."

But even more inspiring than the history and the scenery are the people of this region. They are the warmest, kindest and most honest folk I have come across. I owe my career to so many of them who supported me before, during and after I became MP for Sedgefield – just a few miles from Durham – and then Prime Minister. There was always a friendly face to offer up an opinion about the big issues of the day, to challenge me on my decisions, or just chat over a pint in the Dun Cow Inn in Sedgefield village after a long week in Westminster. I will always be grateful for this friendship and support, and it's one of the reasons my Sports and Faith Foundations work in this region today.

Nowadays my work has a global reach, but I will forever be proud to say I was raised in the North East.

"There was always a friendly face to offer up an opinion about the big issues of the day, to challenge me on my decisions, or just chat over a pint in the Dun Cow Inn in Sedgefield village after a long week in Westminster."

ERIC BURDON

singer and musician

Newcastle-born Eric Burdon is the finest blues singer of his generation. As front-man of the chart-topping group The Animals his fame rivalled that of The Beatles and The Rolling Stones in the Sixties. Now living in California, he is still touring and released the album 'Til Your River Runs Dry *in 2013.*

© Marianna Proestou

ALTHOUGH I GREW UP ON TYNESIDE, most of my summer school holidays were spent in Edinburgh. My uncle was a Regimental Sergeant Major in the Tyneside Scottish Infantry so I was acutely aware of my border heritage. My mother's side of the family came from Ireland, and they moved to Scotland then down to Newcastle during the 1930s industry boom. My mother's side of the family lived in North End, Scotswood Road. My father's side of the family lived on the Tyne Bank, half a mile from Tyne Tees TV. I never got to meet my grandfather on the English side but I found out recently that he was the wheelman on the Swing Bridge on the River Tyne. So that river and myself have a long-standing relationship.

Early school years were a dark nightmare. A combination of the river pollution and humidity led to asthma attacks, which I still encounter today. A little reminder of what I inherited from Newcastle. In primary school I was stuck at the back of a classroom of around 40 to 50 kids and I received constant harassment from kids and teachers alike. This school was jammed between a slaughterhouse and noisy shipyard on the banks of the Tyne.

But later I remember in secondary school a teacher called Bertie Brown was responsible for getting me into art school and changing my world. It was like the heavens opened up. And there were girls, lots of girls! Possibly this didn't help my asthma either. But I did meet John Steel (The Animals' founder drummer) and other young rebels who shared the same interest in jazz, folk and movies. I also met a great gang of older guys called The Squatters, out of which evolved the Pagan Jazz Band.

Picture courtesy of John Steel

A young Eric Burdon with John Steel on drums in their 1958 band The Pagans, with art school pals Philip Payne and Dave Ashcroft on guitar

Folk, jazz and blues sustained us and gave us hope for a new future.

The first 78 record I bought was Johnny Ray's *Cry*, which started me singing in the bathroom. The second was *Shotgun Boogie* by Tennessee Ernie Ford, but the B-side was even better – *16 Tons* recorded in 1941, the year I was born. Then *Shame, Shame, Shame* by Smiley Lewis – I still sing this one today. This song was featured in the movie *Baby Doll*, directed by Eli Kazan and starring Carol Baker. I saw it with many other radical movies at the Stoll Theatre. This venue should be treasured as a true remnant of Tyneside's theatrical history. Then came

"I never got to meet my grandfather on the English side but I found out recently that he was the wheelman on the Swing Bridge on the River Tyne. So that river and myself have a long-standing relationship."

The Animals rivalled The Beatles and The Rolling Stones in their Sixties heyday
Left to right: Eric, Chas Chandler, John Steel, Hilton Valentine and Alan Price

Eric is still touring and making records

a revolution with 45s and jukeboxes in Whitley Bay at the Spanish City. Ray Charles's *What'd I Say* was a big hit. Other American imports we loved were Fats Domino, Elvis, Gene Vincent and Buddy Holly. My friends and I would spend Sundays hanging out with a pocket full of change to feed the machine.

There was also the Tyneside Film Club, right there off Northumberland Street, of which I was member number 27. This is where we could see movies that were banned from general release. There was a coffee shop upstairs where we could hang out and discuss the movies, smoke cigarettes and wish we were James Dean, Rod Steiger and Marlon Brando. We were awakened to the Method school of acting and it fanned our desire to get to New York.

As soon as I finished my art studies, I was offered the job of designing the interior of a club. It became the famous Club A'Gogo. It was my first and only job as a designer in the commercial world. The 'Gogo was a shining star of the northern British club world, which meant it also had to be a den of iniquity. It's where the North East mob was born – they ran several clubs in the area. It was a mixture of teen heaven with the devil running loose wielding a hatchet. It was the only place outside of one club in London that actually had a full-on gaming licence. It was very clear that the mob from London would take interest, as gaming back then was strictly controlled in England. Only one club in London's West End had been allowed the game of roulette. I have many great memories from the 'Gogo. I remember when the late John Lee Hooker played there, he said to me: "Man, I've seen some wild stuff in my years but nothing like this. This is Newcastle, Mississippi."

If my soul resides anywhere, it must be on the road from Newcastle to Lindisfarne. It's cold, mysterious, dark and yet a bright light breaks through the clouds. And there is the imagined fear of invasion. It's truly Northumberland. As for moving back to the North East if I could find a cottage near a stream, with a Border collie, underfloor heating, a large fireplace, a Range Rover outside, a local pub down the road – then I could stand a little drizzle.

www.ericburdon.com

"If my soul resides anywhere, it must be on the road from Newcastle to Lindisfarne. And there is the imagined fear of invasion. It's truly Northumberland."

SIR BOBBY CHARLTON

footballer

Bobby Charlton is one of the greatest forwards and midfield players of all time. He joined Manchester United from school, made his debut in 1956 and in 758 appearances scored 249 goals. One of the famous Busby Babes, after surviving the Munich air disaster he went on to captain the European Cup-winning team in 1968 – two years after winning the World Cup with England. He is now on the board of Manchester United and lives in Cheshire with wife Norma.

I WAS REALLY LUCKY because my mother was a Milburn and her four brothers were all professional footballers. I tried to pick up as much as I could from all of them about how to play the game properly and I spent a lot of time as a kid talking to them about the game. There were my uncles Jimmy, Jack and George who all played for Leeds and Stan for Leicester and Rochdale. Then there was Jackie Milburn, who was my mother's cousin.

I decided at an early age I wanted to be a professional footballer. I didn't find the game difficult at all. My uncles taught me what they knew: they told me what you had to do to be a success and the importance of being fit and playing football fairly.

It was difficult not to support Newcastle with the Milburn blood in your veins.

Jackie was a Geordie who stayed in the area and played for Newcastle United and he was a great favourite with the fans. If my brother Jack and I were fortunate enough to go down to St James' Park on a Saturday to see a First Division match we would sit near the corner flag on the gravel. We loved to watch who was taking the corners. In those days – it was the Fifties – it might be the great Tom Finney or Stanley Matthews. It was magic going to St James' Park.

We didn't have enough money to go to all the Newcastle matches on the bus from Ashington as it was a lot of money in those days. But I loved being Jackie Milburn's nephew. I was so proud of him, especially when he scored at St James' Park – the place went crazy. And he scored an awful lot of goals!

Growing up in Ashington I played for Hirst North A juniors when I was about ten years old then passed the 11-plus and was set to go to Morpeth Grammar. But they didn't play football there – it was more of a rugby school – so my headmaster Mr Hamilton fixed it for me to get into Bedlington Grammar who did have a good football team.

I was football mad. I just wanted to be a footballer so much. I remember once playing for East Northumberland Boys and we had a game near Newcastle somewhere. After the match this little man came shuffling across the pitch. It was Joe Armstrong. He said: "I'm a scout for Manchester United and we'd love to have you there as a player. Think about it." I said: "I've already made my mind up!"

Joining Manchester United was one of the best decisions I have ever made. I wanted to travel and see the world and it worked out for me perfectly. It's been fantastic. I never thought in my wildest dreams I would achieve everything that I did in football. And the club has been fantastic to me.

If Munich was a low-point in my career a high point must have been winning the World Cup in 1966 with brother Jack also in the side. We were very proud of that – two lads from Ashington in the England team that won the World Cup. Although Bobby Robson and I both played county schoolboy football in the North East our paths never crossed then. The first time I met him was when we played for England at under-23 level. He played club football for Fulham when they were at their peak, and we played at senior level for England together around 1960-1. I understood his love of the game and I admired his philosophy. He was a fine player but became a great coach and manager – and a great friend to me. Bobby always wanted to talk football, even just before he died. He was always so generous with his knowledge of the game and was so keen to pass on everything he knew about the great game of football. He was generous of spirit and wanted to share his great knowledge.

When I was growing up we generally took our family holidays in Northumberland – never too far away from home. Northumberland is a beautiful county. I always loved going to the coast. I love the North Sea and we only lived about three miles from it. We would go to places like Bamburgh, Amble and all those lovely villages right up to Berwick on the border. I have very fond memories of those days. Although we grew up in a pit village we were never far away from beautiful countryside.

I remember the first train I ever saw was at Alnmouth – and that spectacular view has stayed with me. We found that the main railway line from Edinburgh to Newcastle ran very close to us so we would get on our bikes and spend hours watching the trains going by. The River Wansbeck was close by too. I have lived away from the North East for most of my life but I still miss the people and the stunning countryside. I don't get back to the North East very much these days because my family and job are in the North West. But I still have two cousins up there, Sheila and Margaret – who are great, great friends – and I always try and see them if I'm back in the region.

"I remember the first train I ever saw was at Alnmouth – and that spectacular view has stayed with me."

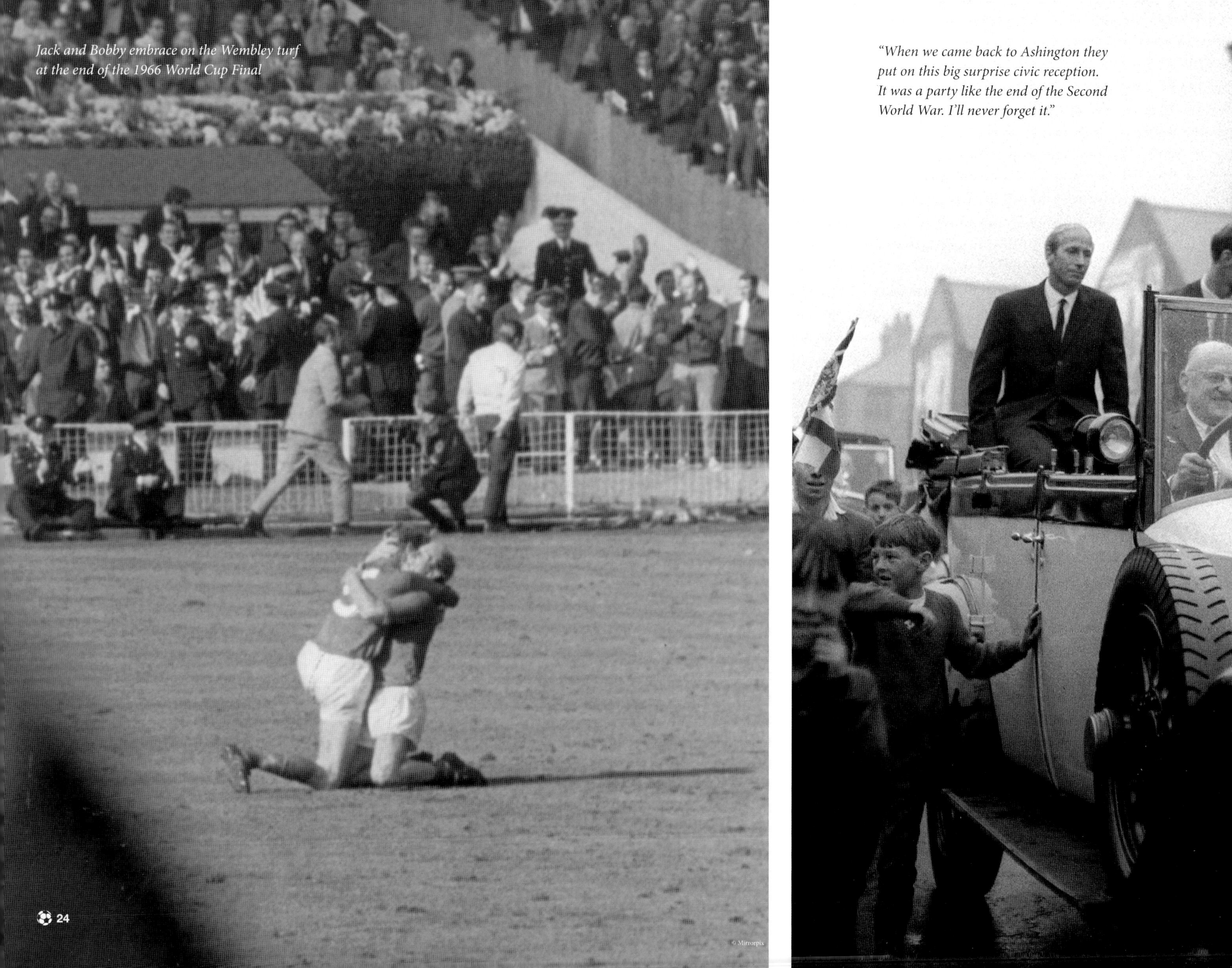

Jack and Bobby embrace on the Wembley turf at the end of the 1966 World Cup Final

"When we came back to Ashington they put on this big surprise civic reception. It was a party like the end of the Second World War. I'll never forget it."

Bobby leans over to greet his mother

JACK CHARLTON OBE

footballer and football manager

Jack Charlton played centre half in the Sixties and Seventies Leeds United side. He made a club record 773 appearances and won 35 England caps, playing in the 1966 England team which won the World Cup with his brother Bobby Charlton. He later managed Middlesbrough, Newcastle and Ireland. He lives near Ponteland with wife Pat.

I FIND IT FUNNY that most people ask me about fishing rather than football. People seem to remember me for my fishing rather than my football achievements even though my wife and I got honorary Irish citizenship after I managed the Ireland team.

I've lived in Dalton near Ponteland for 30 years now, since I managed Newcastle United in the 1984-5 season. Even when I managed Ireland later, the airport is just a few miles away so it's great for me. I've always preferred fishing rivers to reservoirs. From here I can easily go fishing up on the Coquet or the Tweed or the Tyne – all great salmon and trout rivers. I used to fish at Whittle Dene ponds just down the road but it's all coarse fishing there now so I fish at Hallington if the conditions are not good for river fishing.

I've fished ever since I was a lad. When we were growing up in Ashington my uncle Tommy Skinner, who used to drive a delivery wagon for the Co-op, would take us to the other side of Morpeth to Bothal where there was a spring that fed into the Wansbeck. There was great fishing there. Bobby wasn't really into fishing but I remember this one time I put a rod together for him there. I was fishing about 200 yards upstream from him. I heard him shout and he pulled out a good-sized trout weighing about two pounds. But as he lifted it out of the water it dropped off the hook and he said: "I suppose that doesn't count?"

I used to love going to Newbiggin-by-the-Sea as a kid when I was just maybe nine or ten years old. I'd go with my pals and we'd catch mackerel with spinners. The water would be boiling with little fry and the fish would be biting like crazy. We'd catch them, take them home and eat them. I once caught a big cod there and took it home for my mother to cook for the family.

We were always playing football as kids. In primary school it would be with a tennis ball in the yard. Later I played in the East Northumberland League, which was one of the strongest for under-16s. Scouts from all the professional clubs would come and watch. Bobby was 15 when he went to Manchester United and I went to Leeds. My uncle Jimmy was still playing for Leeds when I joined them. Before that I worked at the pit – Linton Colliery – for a few months. I actually enjoyed it. I didn't do anything dangerous. I would put the tickets on the coal wagons when they weighed them. I was all set to join the police force after that but on the day I got an interview at Morpeth I'd already been asked to go for a trial to Leeds – funnily enough against Newcastle United. So I missed my chance to join the police!

Bob and I loved going to St James' Park to watch Newcastle as kids and see our cousin Jackie Milburn play. We'd normally go on our own because we didn't want to bother Jackie on match day but if he saw us he would make sure we could sit right behind where the trainers were on the touchline. After the match we'd go to watch the wrestling at St James' Hall then get the bus back to Ashington where our parents would meet us off the bus. There was always a car waiting to take Jackie home after the game but if he wasn't ready to go straight home Bob and I would get to take the taxi all the way home. What a treat that was.

When Bob was at Manchester United and I was at Leeds I would come back to Ashington most weekends. Bob didn't come back as much as me but if we did come home on the same weekend I'd make sure I got on his train as it came through Leeds and we'd travel home together.

We were so proud to be in the England team that won the World Cup in 1966. It was unusual for two brothers to be in the same team anyway but to be in the same side that won the World Cup was unbelievable. I remember when the final whistle went Bob and I were on our knees on the Wembley pitch hugging each other. Everybody was smiling but he was crying. He said: "That's it, there's nowt for us to win now!"

When we came back to Ashington they put on this big surprise civic reception. The streets were full of people cheering and shouting our names as we rode in a yellow open-top Rolls-Royce with flags and bunting lining the streets. It was a party like the end of the Second World War. I'll never forget it.

"I loved to go to Newbiggin-by-the-Sea when I was a lad. I'd go with my pals and we would catch mackerel with spinners. The water would be boiling with little fry and the fish would be biting like crazy."

CHARLIE CHARLTON

radio and TV presenter

Charlie Charlton co-presents The Breakfast Show *on BBC Radio Newcastle with Alfie Joey and has worked on the programme for ten years. Her TV interviews for BBC Newcastle have also featured on* Panorama *and* Newsnight. *She lives in Low Fell, Gateshead and is a patron of two charities – the Cyrenians and Newcastle Toy Leisure Library.*

SALTWELL PARK IS A REAL HIDDEN GEM – it's the finest example of a Victorian park in Britain. I adore it because it has everything you would want. The fabulous centrepiece is Saltwell Towers, where William Wailes – the famous stained-glass expert – used to live. And he later sold it to Gateshead Council. It has amazing architecture and a Japanese garden commissioned by Nissan, which is surreal in itself. There is a lovely café, a yew tree maze, a dene with a beautiful stream, a four-acre boating lake and stunning ornamental and woodland gardens.

Most of my childhood was spent playing there. It had a real aeroplane in it in those days and you could sit at the controls and pretend you were flying it. Then you could actually slide down the emergency chute to escape too! I love hearing musicians bring the bandstand to life, and watching the Canada geese fly in on their migration trail. I love it so much I actually carry pictures of it around with me.

I love the whole of the North East but another special place is the fabulous Northumberland coastline up near Low Newton. My friend has one of those huts there – the ones without electricity – which you can't get for love nor money. What a great place to stay. If I have friends up from London I take them up to Craster and Dunstanburgh with that idyllic stretch of sand. The expanse of it all is breathtaking. I particularly love it when the weather is terrible and you can just sit and watch the clouds rolling in – it's like a giant tidal wave in the sky. You could be the world's worst artist and still paint a flawless picture of that.

I was born and bred in Gateshead and went to primary school there before going to school in Newcastle. Everyone there was from Jesmond and Gosforth and they told me I was from the wrong side of the Tyne, darling! I then went to university in London and lived there and overseas for years but the pull back to the North East was just too strong, so I'm back in Low Fell again with family and friends nearby.

I'm a real fan of the *Get Carter* movie. I'm not wild about brutalist architecture but I loved the Trinity Square car park with the restaurant at the top, which featured in the film and which they later pulled down. I've got pictures of it all over my house. My grandparents actually lived in Coburg Street in Gateshead, which they used for the guesthouse scene where Michael Caine comes out naked – in that terraced street with all the washing hanging out – and chases off two hitmen.

I always thought I would end up in business because my parents left school and worked in their own offshore and haulage business. But I went travelling after university and that was when I decided I wanted to do broadcast journalism. So I did a post-graduate course at the London College of Printing and got the chance to come home to Radio Newcastle. I started doing reporting shifts and news-reading then moved to presenting the breakfast show and I've been there ten years now. I can't really see me moving away. Where else can you get this quality of life and how do you put a price on it?

When I moved to London and went to University College I ended up in a hall of residence with all these incredibly posh people. I became their comedy Geordie friend. What they all agree on now is how friendly everyone is here. When a group of friends came up from London, they went to a pub in the city centre whilst I was at work in the newsroom. They presumed they'd stumbled across my local, because everyone at the bar started to strike up a conversation. They soon realised that's just the way we are up here – nosy and hilarious raconteurs!

The 'Get Carter' *car park in Gateshead*

I love travelling around the world and meeting people – that's my passion. South America is about the only country I haven't really explored. So I get really excited about going away but I always love coming back home.

www.bbc.co.uk/bbcnewcastle

"I love hearing musicians bring the Saltwell Park bandstand to life, and watching the Canada geese fly in on their migration trail."
Saltwell Towers – the centrepiece of Saltwell Park

GEORGE CLARKE

architect, TV presenter and writer

Born in Sunderland and educated at Newcastle University, George fulfilled his childhood dream to become an architect after graduating in 1995. Since 2004 he has presented a series of TV programmes including Property Dreams, The Home Show, The Restoration Man *and* George Clarke's Amazing Spaces. *He lives in West London with his wife and three children.*

I LOVED GROWING UP IN THE NORTH EAST. I was born in Sunderland but my mam and dad moved to Washington when I was only two or three. It was a new town, a new-build council estate, a new way of living. It was an amazing place to grow up. A lot of people are quite critical of new towns but I didn't know anything else. People say Washington is faceless – all roundabouts and districts. I lived in District Three which sounds very Orwellian but when you lived there you didn't refer to the districts. I lived in Blackfell and friends lived in Albany. That's the way you talked about it when you lived there. I could walk to Blackfell Junior School from my house – which was about two miles – without crossing a road. Even when I went to Oxclose Comprehensive I only had to cross a couple of roads. I still think the way it was planned was genius. It felt incredibly safe. I remember the streets were all pedestrianised and it was very green.

I'm a big Sunderland fan so my Saturdays were taken up watching my football team. My grandparents lived in Fulwell then. In fact all my aunties and uncles and family still live in Sunderland. I went to my first match at Roker Park in 1985 when I was 11. My uncle took me and after that I never missed a home game for years. Even when I got my first Saturday job I made sure I was finished at 1pm then I'd get the bus to Roker Park. It was £1.50 to get in and I used to stand in exactly the same spot in the Roker end every week and have a Bovril and a pie at half-time. The team was rubbish in the late Eighties but they were all superheroes to me. It was the era of players like Gary Bennett, Marco Gabbiadini and Eric Gates. I was obsessed. My bedroom was painted red and I used to spend my pocket money on pictures of the players at 50p a time. You would buy them from a tiny SAFC shop next to Jacky White's market. It was the Holy Grail to me. I know it's all changed for the better with the Premiership but I feel proud and privileged to be part of that football generation.

"I used to stand in exactly the same spot in the Roker end every week and have a Bovril and a pie at half-time."

I loved being close to the coast too – I like Seaburn a lot – and have fond memories of caravan holidays in Redcar. We never ventured that far from home. We certainly never went abroad for holidays. We didn't have the money for it. I remember the first time we went on a family holiday to Spain it was to the Costa Brava. We went on the bus and stayed in a tent. It never bothered

"Durham Cathedral embodies what the North East is about."

me. Summer holidays were great at home playing football with your mates and kicking around the doors.

When I qualified as an architect I used to work for Terry Fowler Partners on Newcastle Quayside. That's where I trained and Sir Terry was involved in the master plan. Look what's happened there. It's fantastic and Gateshead is brilliant, absolutely phenomenal. There's a real buzz about the place.

Durham Cathedral was a massive inspiration: it's the best building in the world. I'm obviously massively biased but it's 1,000 years old and it's beautiful but strong. It was built at an exciting time. We had just come out of the Dark Ages. It blows me away now, so imagine what it must have been like to have walked up that hill and set eyes on it 1,000 years ago. Any time I am on the train back home I can't wait for that moment when the carriage pulls into Durham station and you glimpse the Cathedral for the first time.

We don't shout about it enough. When I was about 13 or 14 I remember getting on the bus with my sketchpad. I spent the whole day sketching it and I knew I'd never be anything other than an architect.

Durham Cathedral embodies what the North East is about. I'm not a religious person but I defy anyone not to be moved by the spirituality of the place. I'm so passionate about its history – Bede, Cuthbert and the Lindisfarne Gospels. It sounds like a contradiction but it would make my life if I could be buried there. I feel that strongly connected to it.

I live in London now and that's my second home but I still miss the people, the grittiness of the area and the landscape of County Durham and Northumberland. Wherever I travel in the world people hear my accent and they say: "You're from the North East. What lovely people they are." What an international brand and recommendation that is.

www.georgeclarke.com

"Durham Cathedral was a massive inspiration. It is the best building in the world. It sounds like a contradiction but it would make my life if I could be buried there. I feel that strongly connected to it."

PAUL COLLINGWOOD MBE

cricketer

Paul Collingwood is one of the finest cricketers England has produced. He played 300 matches for England after making his debut in 2003 and went on to captain the one-day side. His first-class cricket began at Durham County Cricket Club in 1996. He now captains the side in the LV= County Championship. A three-time Ashes winner, Collingwood led England to win the 2010 World Twenty20.

© Your Sports Photography

I WAS BORN WITH A COMPETITIVE STREAK. For nearly all of my youth I was trying to beat my older brother Peter, whether it was at cricket, football, fashion or whatever. Being older, he would always win but it never stopped me trying. I think that helped give me an edge later when I became a professional sportsman.

Cricket was something that my whole family was involved in for as long as I can remember. We lived at Shotley Bridge and the cricket club there was where we seemed to spend most of our time during my childhood. My dad used to play, my brother was a team captain and my mother was a tea lady. So I didn't really have much choice about whether cricket would be in my life, but I know that's what I'd have chosen anyway.

Durham became a first-class cricket county in 1992 and I made my debut in 1996. Playing cricket at the Riverside Stadium in Chester-le-Street in the sunshine with a great crowd watching and Lumley Castle in the background is always a fantastic experience, and I'm privileged to play for the county where I'm from.

For any sportsperson, the ultimate has to be playing for your country. For me, playing in Test matches and gaining Test caps is the thing I'm proudest of – everything else after that is a bonus.

Some of the things that my success in cricket has brought me have been almost surreal: going to Buckingham Palace to collect my MBE, going to the Prime Minister's house, carrying the Olympic torch through Durham – sometimes you have to pinch yourself to make sure it's not a dream.

When you realise where it started – at a local cricket club – it can seem like a long journey but, the more I think about it the more I believe that the grounding you get at places like that is what makes you what you are. It's amazing what Shotley Bridge Cricket Club taught me in terms of values. It's not just about the people in whites on the pitch – it's about all the volunteers who make it happen. They're not professional, they don't get paid, but without people like my dad cutting the field, the groundsmen, the people who look after the clubhouse, the ladies like my mother making teas then none of it would be possible.

So Shotley Bridge will always be an important place to me, as that's where I spent all my childhood. Now I've moved to the Tyne Valley and I love it round there, with places like Corbridge which is so beautiful. We're spoilt for choice in the North East. I think back to Alnmouth where we used to go for day trips when I was young and the whole coast up to Bamburgh – it's fantastic. This region is a bit of a hidden gem, and I would like to keep it that way!

Another favourite place for me as a Sunderland fan is the Stadium of Light. I remember meeting Sir Bobby Robson there at an international and he was chatting away merrily to the punters, really enjoying himself. He's the epitome of the best of the North East character and I have great respect for him.

www.durhamccc.co.uk

© Durham CCC

"Playing cricket at the Riverside Stadium in Chester-le-Street in the sunshine with a great crowd watching and Lumley Castle in the background is always a fantastic experience."

Emirates Durham International Cricket Ground

"I've moved to the Tyne Valley and I love it round there, with places like Corbridge which is so beautiful."

KAT COPELAND MBE

rower

A professional rower and key member of the Tees Rowing Club, Kat won a gold medal in the women's lightweight double sculls in the London 2012 Olympics with her rowing partner Sophie Hosking. Kat was voted joint North East Sports Personality of the Year with swimmer Josef Craig and was awarded an MBE.

LOOKING AT ME AS A TEENAGER at secondary school you'd never think I was cut out to be a professional athlete. I was a bit chubby, quite self-conscious and not really into sport at all.

It all started when I went on a cross-country run with my school. There were about 100 people in my year and I came second last. I decided to get fit and I started going running – just so I wouldn't do so badly the following year.

I became more and more interested in sport, but got into rowing by chance at the age of 14 as one of my friends did it and needed someone to row with her. I said yes and we started in the summer. It was nice and hot and it didn't matter that we were falling into the river half the time! But I was very keen to train and make progress and, when I was about 16, I got into competitive rowing and did some junior trials.

I was really enjoying it and wanted to give it a year or so to see how good I could get. That's about the age a lot of people drop out. Rowing is very demanding and it wasn't the coolest thing you could do! At that age most people just want to have nights out and enjoy themselves, but I was determined to keep going.

I was doing well and I decided to move to London because I thought that's where all the best rowers were, so I had to be there. It just didn't work out for me and I nearly quit, but I spoke to James Harris, a great coach at Tees Rowing Club, and he built up my confidence and convinced me to carry on. He has been a real inspiration. He actually confided to my boyfriend in 2011 that he thought I could go on to win an Olympic gold medal, but neither of them said anything to me!

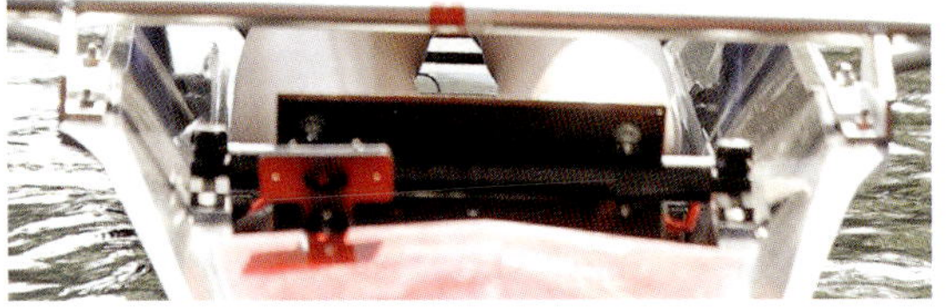

Sophie and I weren't favourites to win gold, so when it happened it was incredible. I had this strange feeling of relief as well as happiness when we crossed the line. The photo of me hugging Sophie has been seen everywhere, but funnily it felt like a very private moment to me, as she and I had been through a lot together.

Later being awarded the MBE was amazing. My mum was absolutely buzzing. You never think anything like that is going to happen to you, so it's pretty cool: quite random but really special.

I definitely have Tees Rowing Club and the people there to thank for a lot of my success. The Tees is special to me and I love seeing the Infinity Bridge at Stockton where we start and finish training.

Although I was born in Ashington we moved to Ingleby Barwick when I was three, and I still live near there so that's where most of my memories are. I remember as a kid my father would make us walk around the Cleveland Hills, whatever the weather was like. We'd be trudging along through hailstones and we hated it but now I think it's beautiful and I enjoy taking my dogs for walks round there. I also like the industrial landscape of the Stockton area. It may not be everybody's idea of a great view, but the sight of all the big chimneys makes me feel at home.

"I love seeing the Infinity Bridge at Stockton where we start and finish training."

JOSEF CRAIG MBE

swimmer

Great Britain's youngest gold medal winner in the 2012 Paralympics at the age of 15, Josef, who has cerebral palsy, went on to win North East Sports Personality of the Year (with Olympic rower Kat Copeland) then BBC Young Sports Personality of the Year. In his honour, a postbox was painted gold in his hometown of Jarrow and he is featured on a stamp.

I WASN'T HAPPY ON MY BIRTHDAY in February 2012. I was walking down the street with my mum and she asked me what was wrong. I said: "I'm 15 years old today. That's a fifth of my life gone and what have I got to show for it?" Now, when I think of all the things that happened in the months after that, I can hardly get my head round it.

Winning the gold medal in the 400 metres freestyle in the Paralympics and breaking my own world record was just unbelievable – I certainly hadn't expected it. Standing on the podium with the National Anthem playing was my proudest moment so far.

Receiving an MBE was also fantastic. I'm a very patriotic person, and I've always had a great love for the Royal Family, so meeting the Queen and having her talk to me like a friend was surreal.

Then there were the two sports awards. Just amazing. I have to say, the weather may not have been any different to normal during that time, but the days seemed a lot more sunny after that gold medal.

Another great moment for me was switching on the Christmas lights in Newcastle in November 2012. I was over the moon. One of the national newspapers gave star ratings to the different celebrities around the UK and only Rihanna was rated higher than me!

But if anyone thinks I have let this go to my head, they'd be wrong. If you called me a star it just wouldn't be right. There are so many people behind me in the North East and so much of what I've achieved is as much down to them as myself. I had a stage when I wasn't sure that swimming was for me. I felt a bit stressed and pressured but they got me through it.

As well as my family and friends, my school – St Joseph's in Hebburn – has always been really supportive. They never say 'no' to someone who wants to achieve something. They help you catch up academically. It's such a great environment.

In swimming itself, I've had three great coaches who have been an absolute inspiration. The first was Dot Houston at South Tyneside Swimming Club. She physically picked me up when I walked towards the slow lane. She said: "You're better than that" and put me in the fast lane.

Then there was Ken Nesworthy who had a massive impact on me. He was like a second father and it was a privilege to have known him. He taught me that natural ability can only get you so far. If you only put in 50 per cent of effort, then that's what you get back. You have to put in 100 per cent to get anywhere. Without his support I wouldn't be where I am today, simple as. He's moved away from the area now but I still keep in touch.

The third person is my current coach Paul Robinson, an able-bodied athlete and swimmer himself. He's more like a mate as well as a coach but he trains me damn hard!

Apart from swimming, one of the greatest loves of my life is Newcastle United. After the Paralympics Alan Pardew, Demba Ba and Steve Harper did a video link to the school to say 'well done', which I thought was a true act of kindness. Then I was asked to some matches and to watch a few training sessions. I really enjoyed it, both as a Geordie and a Toon fan.

I was quite young when Sir Bobby Robson was the manager, but I remember him well. There's someone

Josef celebrates winning a gold medal

who is a true legend and inspiration – not just to Geordies but to Sunderland and Middlesbrough fans too, and just about everyone who loves football.

Newcastle itself means a lot to me. Whenever I've been away swimming abroad and I come back home and see the Tyne Bridge, I know I'm home. It just gleams and shines and I love it. Seeing the Tyne and the bridges as you're coming into Newcastle – I can't think of anything more wonderful.

"Seeing the Tyne and the bridges as you're coming into Newcastle – I can't think of anything more wonderful."

GRAEME DANBY

classical singer

An operatic bass who has performed at leading opera houses including the Royal Opera House, English National Opera in London and La Scala in Milan, Graeme Danby is also a tutor at the University of Sunderland. He was educated at the Royal Academy of Music in London.

ST JAMES' PARK IS A WORLD AWAY from the biggest operatic and concert stages where I usually ply my trade, but it's a joy to perform there. Singing in front of more than 52,000 people there is a great feeling – especially singing *The Blaydon Races*, an anthem close to my heart. Newcastle United is my team and has been for the whole of my life, but I still want all of the North East teams to do well. I don't make myself very popular for saying that, but I feel it's really important for the region.

My memories of the North East are varied and mostly very happy. I was born in Shotley Bridge and we lived in East Law near Consett, then on to Flint Hill and in 1977 we moved to Darras Hall.

As a youngster I loved sport and music in equal measure, which meant there was never a dull moment for my mum and dad who acted as a never-ending taxi service to football, rugby, the Consett Junior Citizens choir and piano and singing lessons. Golf is the sport I love playing these days. My parents remain a powerful force in my life. I speak to them every day and enjoy the fact that they are still relatively healthy and able to live life well.

We very rarely took holidays in the North East but regular days out mean my knowledge of the region is extensive. From Seahouses to Kielder, Stanhope to South Shields, Hexham to Alnmouth – our region has so much to offer both tourists and residents. Special places for me include Wallington Hall, Sunderland Minster, the Memorial Hall in Ponteland, Consett Empire Theatre, St James' Park – and Dipton Colliery Junior School!

If I had to pick a favourite place, though, it would probably be Ponteland Methodist Church where my wife Valerie and I were married. She is my rock, soul mate and best friend without whom none of the successes and challenges of the last 20 years would have been remotely possible.

I also have a particular soft spot for St Nicholas' Cathedral in Newcastle. I was a boy chorister there at ten years old – it cemented my love of singing and my admiration of cathedral acoustics.

Newcastle, a cornerstone of the industrial revolution, is one of the few big cities in Britain from which, within 20 minutes, you can be in glorious countryside or by the sea. It's vibrant but earthy. For me, Newcastle never gets above itself – it's always welcoming and warm. My gratitude to the loyal audience of the region who support me in so many ways is beyond words.

Living in the North East would be tricky as work determines where I have to be at the minute – but never say never. The areas near the sea at Alnmouth, Dunstanburgh and Craster sound very tempting.

Whatever happens, I have strong ties to the region which will last forever. There are some great people who have inspired me, from the bass singer Owen Brannigan who came from Northumberland and the songwriter Eric Boswell to the rugby maestro Rob Andrew.

I hope I can be a bit of an inspiration too. In 2008 I put into place changes in my professional life that would take me into the university sector (first at Northumbria University and now at the University of Sunderland) which holds a very special place in my heart. I'm completely taken up with what I have to do, bringing on youngsters in the same field. I'm grateful to them and they're grateful, too: it's a 50-50 relationship.

Graeme as Pooh Bah in The Mikado *at the ENO*

It's given me an insight into what it's like to be a young person starting out and how much work you have to do to make it in a tough and crowded market. I try to give them the knowledge to help them travel down that path. It's not an easy one.

The chance to teach and hopefully shape the music and performing talent of the future is very exciting. The balance between performing on the world's stages and platforms with mentoring and teaching provides me with a very nice diary headache. Long may it continue.

"I was a boy chorister at St Nicholas' Cathedral in Newcastle at ten years old – it cemented my love of singing and my admiration of cathedral acoustics."

SIMON DONALD

stand-up comedian and co-founder of cult comic Viz

Simon Donald and brother Chris were the masterminds behind the Viz comic phenomenon. Created in their bedroom in Newcastle in 1979, it went on to top a million sales. Simon now lives in Highgate, North London and is forging a career as a stand-up comedian.

THE VIEW OF BAMBURGH CASTLE from the beach is a favourite of mine. My happiest times as a small boy were spent on the Northumberland coast. In the late Sixties we began having family summer holidays in a little village called Low Buston near Warkworth. The cottage belonged to the Davidson family who had a jeweller's shop on Grey Street in Newcastle and were friends of my mam. From Low Buston we would have day trips to Bamburgh and spend the day on the beach. If you grow up with that as your starting point it tends to spoil you for anywhere else – a beautiful beach of golden sand and a majestic castle.

I remember my mam had a swish metal red-and-white folding picnic table and chairs that collapsed neatly to become its own carrying case. She would prepare endless cups of tea, sandwiches and cake while me and my brothers Chris and Steve would spend hours just mucking around on the beach with our buckets and spades. My dad was a keen photographer and he took terrific colour slides of it all, which was really unusual for that time.

We began doing the Viz comic at home in 16 Lily Crescent in Jesmond, but the place that it first went on sale was above the Gosforth Hotel in the function room where the bands used to play – and that was where Mr Sting's career began with Last Exit.

Newcastle at that time was great. It had a really vibrant arts scene – there were musicians, poets and artists who seemed to have the same sort of collective sensibility. Punk rock had exploded onto the scene around 1976 and this was three years later.

We were in this post-punk scene driven by the mentality that you could do it yourself – you didn't have to have a corporate giant behind you to succeed. And we all promoted each other's work. The bands at the Gosforth Hotel were very supportive of us and allowed us to sell Viz there.

Simon (middle) with Chris (left) and Steve (right)

Then we all moved down to the Quayside around 1980 and Arthur 2 Stroke – which was one of the most influential bands of the time – took up residency at the Cooperage pub. It's so sad to see that closed now. Another piece of great Newcastle history has gone.

The bands of the time all used to practise in this cheap rehearsal room on the corner of Broad Chare – it was a rat-infested den where you could make as much noise as you liked. And we all used to drink in the Baltic wine cellar next door, which was full of dodgy gangster-looking types. But the beer was cheap and they had a pool table so we loved it. In those days the Quayside was virtually deserted. It was before the Quayside Development Corporation started the regeneration programme. So when I look back at my youth it felt like we really were in at the start of this vibrant regeneration. I'm proud to see how it has developed.

The Cooperage pub

It sounds like a cliché but I really miss how friendly the people are in the North East. Fortunately I'm lucky enough to get back there fairly frequently with my stand-up act, so I get a regular 'fix' of friendly people to keep me going.

A lot of people knock what Newcastle has become as one of the party cities of the world, but why not? What was the city supposed to do if all the heavy industry was closed down? At least we have created a place with fantastic venues like the Live Theatre, the Sage, the Baltic and all the great bars and restaurants to attract the tourists and day-trippers to come and spend money on Tyneside.

Unfortunately that has left the Bigg Market as the hen and stag party capital of Europe but at least you know where to go to avoid them.

 www.simondonald.com

"When I look back at my youth it feels like we really were in at the start of this vibrant regeneration of Newcastle Quayside."

BRYAN FERRY CBE

singer, musician and songwriter

As an art student in Newcastle, Bryan was fascinated by music as well as art and he hit the big time with his ground-breaking band Roxy Music in the 1970s. He is now known around the world as a solo artist.

I WENT TO WASHINGTON GRAMMAR SCHOOL and I had a wonderful time there, especially when I reached the sixth form and could concentrate on the subjects I really liked: Art, English and History. The teachers there were incredibly supportive of my talent and eccentricities.

I used to go as often as I could to the City Hall in Newcastle. The first band I saw there was Chris Barber's Jazz Band, but the first concert I remember seeing was Bill Haley and His Comets, which was at Sunderland Empire. I won two front-row seats from a Radio Luxembourg competition and I took my big sister.

I bought my first records at Windows in the Central Arcade off Grey Street in Newcastle. I spent many an hour gazing longingly through their window at their musical instruments and record sleeves. I remember they had little booths where you could go and listen to the record first before buying it. As you can imagine many an hour was spent in there testing out albums I couldn't afford! I had a Saturday job at Jackson the Tailor in Northumberland Street so Windows record shop became a regular place for me to visit.

After school I decided to study Fine Art, and was encouraged to go to Newcastle University rather than go to London and it was the best thing I ever did. For the first time I met other people of my own age who shared the same interests in art and music and I was very lucky to study under the great English Pop artist Richard Hamilton.

There was this connection between the Newcastle fine arts department and the American artists, which

Roxy Music

made it feel special.

I also had this classic American car, a Studebaker. It was a beautiful machine. I think I spent more time pushing it than driving it because it was always conking out. But just to look at it was enough for me. I used to live in Eslington Terrace in Jesmond and had it parked outside.

We used to spend a lot of time at the famous Club A'Gogo in Newcastle, which was the hot scene at the time, and where I saw lots of great bands perform, and where I perfected my dance moves!

While I was at university I put together my own band called The Gas Board and we played a lot of clubs

Bryan with his Studebaker

in the area, playing mainly R 'n' B covers. Two of the musicians from that band – Graham Simpson and John Porter – were later to play with me in Roxy Music, so this was a very important time for me.

After I graduated in 1968 and moved to London I started to put together the band that was to become Roxy Music. I was very fortunate to find a great bunch of people, all as inexperienced as myself, and one of them was a fellow Geordie, Paul Thompson. I put an advert in the music paper Melody Maker and Paul turned up for an audition straight from his job on the building site, and I took to him immediately. He became an integral

"My favourite North East view is Penshaw Monument which I used to see every day from my house in Washington where I grew up."

part of the group.

In my opinion, Newcastle was always a cool place, and in my student years there were two clothes shops where everybody hung out. One of them was called City Stylish, and the other more upmarket store was called Marcus Price.

Marcus was one of the great characters of Newcastle at that time, and a big jazz fan. I think the club culture of Newcastle then was a big part of everyone's obsession with fashion, and one of the places I frequented was the New Orleans Jazz Club where the standard of musicianship and clothing was extremely high. I remember seeing Eric Burdon of The Animals singing there, and there was a great sax player called Nigel Stanger who was later to become a great friend of mine.

I am very pleased to see there is a flourishing arts scene up there and it's great that so much of it is centred around the Quayside, which is the heart and soul of the city. I've always seen Newcastle as a very special city – the architecture is much better than other big cities outside London.

I have four sons (Otis, Isaac, Tara and Merlin) and I have always made them very aware of my and their North East heritage. They are staunch supporters of Newcastle United football team but I do wish they had more direct contact with the area. Luckily my uncle Bryan, after whom I was named, has taught them some good North East values!

I have lived in London since 1968, but I still feel that the North East is my spiritual home. It's a very true saying that you can take a boy out of the North but you can't take the North out of the boy.

My favourite North East view is Penshaw Monument which I used to see every day from my house in Washington where I grew up. I sometimes fantasise that I could one day end up back in the North, probably on a farm in the Border country, which is I think one of the best places in the world.

www.bryanferry.com

Bryan on Penshaw Monument

"I bought my first records at Windows in the Central Arcade."

PETER FLANNERY

playwright and screenwriter

Peter Flannery is best known for his 1996 BBC TV epic drama Our Friends in the North, *for which he won a BAFTA Award for outstanding achievement in television writing, and the BBC TV detective drama* Inspector George Gently, *which is set and filmed on location in the North East.*

I WAS BORN AND BRED IN JARROW and my memories of growing up in the late Fifties and early Sixties were very much about being out of the centre of things and craving a big city life. I was 13 in 1964 and I was desperate to live in a big city, which I later got when I went to university and actually found out I didn't like it very much!

Inspector George Gently is set in Durham and Northumberland in the Sixties – and was actually born in the North East. Ten years had gone by since *Our Friends in the North* in 1996 and I had written lots of stuff for television that didn't make it so I said to myself: "What do they want? Detectives. I'll go and find one." That took me to Barter Books in Alnwick – one of the largest second-hand bookshops in the UK – where I stumbled across the Gently stories written by Alan Hunter. His stories were set in Suffolk but I wanted to film it in the North East.

Ironically, for funding reasons, we had to film the first two series in Dublin, which made no sense at all. You can imagine the difficulty of trying to make a little church in Dublin look like Durham Cathedral. Then we got funding from the regional screen agency Northern Film Media and One North East to bring it back home in 2010 and I was delighted.

The show seemed very settled as soon as we got to Durham and it radically improved it to be set where it was intended, with authentic landscapes and accents. At the end of series five for the *Gently in the Cathedral* episode we actually spent a whole day filming in Durham Cathedral. It culminated with Gently and Bacchus lying at death's door with gunshots ringing out throughout the Cathedral. I was quite surprised that we got the amount of leeway we did to film there. I thought they might object to guns in the Lord's house. It's all blanks of course, but even so everything had to be done in a way so as not to damage all the ancient masonry.

I set Gently in the Sixties because I think the country changed a lot from the mid-Sixties. Culturally there was a huge change, a revolution in music, fashion and pop culture. Swinging Britain was partly born on the crest of that wave of teenagers having money to spend and an identity for the first time. Then there were the great liberal reforms of that Wilson government which brought about legalised abortion, legalised homosexuality and did away with capital punishment.

I wanted to set it just before all that was coming because it has not been a complete blessing. It brought about a diminishing of respect for authority, which seemed like a brilliant idea at the time. It seemed like a great idea, this loosening of respect for authority, sweeping away the old, but then look at the bloody mess the country's got itself into.

The joy of writing the Gently stories lies in the period and the place: the place because it's where I grew up – the period for the same reason. It gives me a chance to write about a country on the cusp of change. And one of the other great things is that it gets me back to the North East again. I would like to shoot a lot more in Northumberland but Durham is easier in many ways because the city centre has remained virtually unchanged for years as it is a World Heritage site. It works well for the Sixties setting, but we have also filmed in Newcastle, Jarrow, South Shields and in the surrounding countryside.

Martin Shaw as Inspector George Gently at Durham Castle. Since 2010 the series has been shot entirely on location in the North East.

I now live in Wallingford, Oxfordshire but I still like to retreat to a little cottage in the hamlet of High Buston, looking down on Alnmouth, to do some writing. It's a great spot when I need to get some peace and quiet to finish off my writing work. It makes it easy to see my mum too. My folks are still up there although I haven't had a place of my own in the North East since I left home to go to university. I still find myself drawn to Marsden Rock every time I'm home. I grew up there, played on the beach there as a kid. I had my first camping holiday there as a teenager. I still love it. There are prettier places in the North East but it's iconic for me.

"I still find myself drawn to Marsden Rock every time I'm home. It's iconic for me because I grew up there."

Marsden Rock pictured before the arch collapsed in 1996

TOBY FLOOD

rugby player

Toby Flood is a key member of the Leicester Tigers squad, England's biggest and most successful rugby club. He has been part of two Premiership-winning squads and won the LV= Cup in 2012. Capped many times by England, he was part of the England squad in the 2007 World Cup Final and represented England at the 2011 World Cup.

THE STAGE WAS NEVER FOR ME, although both of my parents worked in the theatre in the North East – my father recently as manager of the Customs House in South Shields. I hated the idea of having to perform, of putting on a show, although by the age of 15 I'd seen more local theatre productions than most people see in a lifetime. I still love going to see plays, but strictly as a member of the audience.

So I suppose it's ironic that I ended up being a sportsman because obviously, to have a professional career, you do have to do your work in public. But I'm very task-focused when I'm playing rugby: I just think about what's going on on the pitch and don't let anything distract me from the game.

I started my professional career with Newcastle Falcons which was great as I was near home and surrounded by all my friends. Those teenage years have the best memories for me – being around Newcastle at that age when everything was new and fresh.

I started playing rugby very early. My dad used to take me along to Alnwick to train and I loved it but I also loved playing football so I flipped back and forth a bit. In the end I decided to stick with rugby, largely for the social side of it, even though I was so young. At the time we lived in the middle of nowhere and I wanted to see people. After training sessions we'd get hot-dogs and go tearing round the clubhouse together. With football the boys would just be driven home straight after training.

We moved around a lot in my childhood, to Warkworth, Alnwick, Witton Shields – which is very remote and a few miles from Morpeth – and Tynemouth.

I was a free-range kid, spending all my time outside,

Toby in action for the Tigers

free to run everywhere and play by rivers and lakes – and it was encouraged. The front door would open and I'd be ejected out of it! I wouldn't change where I grew up for anything.

Now that I live away from the area what I miss most are the rolling hills and the warm, welcoming people. I think the fact that the North East is so remote and isolated means the people are unique. I think they're a very positive race. When things go wrong they just shrug their shoulders and get on with life. I admire that quality.

One of the first things I do when I go back home is go down to the sea at Tynemouth, to Longsands Beach where I used to go when I was growing up, to surf, walk the dog and just enjoy the sea and the fresh air.

 www.leicestertigers.com

"Longsands Beach is where I used to go when I was growing up, to surf, walk the dog and just enjoy the sea and the fresh air."

BRENDAN FOSTER CBE

athlete and TV commentator

Brendan Foster competed in three Olympic Games, winning bronze in the 10,000 metres in 1976. In 1974 he won gold in the 5,000 metres in the European Championship and broke the world record for the 3,000 metres on his home track Gateshead International Stadium. Since retiring in 1980 he has worked as a commentator for BBC TV and launched the Great North Run in 1981.

I LIVE IN STOCKSFIELD NOW and apart from a year in the States when I worked for Nike I've lived most of my life in the North East. I'm a season ticket holder at St James' Park so I love sitting on the terraces watching Newcastle United. I knew Sir Bobby Robson very well. He started the Great North Run for us in 2007. I would bump into him often at the ground and he would always chat. He was a top man. I remember when I got my CBE in 2008, a few weeks before he came up to me at the match and said: "Have you had your letter yet?" I didn't know what he was on about but he told me there was something big coming my way. He knew long before I did.

I grew up in Hebburn right next to the River Tyne and every morning at 8am I'd see thousands of men arriving to work at Hawthorn Leslie shipyard. Then at 5pm the buzzer would sound, the doors would open and they'd all run up the hill, finished work for the day. When a ship was launched we used to get the day off school. The ship would block the entire bottom of the street as it was being built, then it was launched and would disappear down the river, before work started on another one.

Football was my sport at junior school and I played in the under-11 team with Geordie Armstrong who ended up playing in that great Arsenal double-winning team in 1971. I started running when I went to St Joseph's Grammar. I would play football on a Saturday morning then run for Gateshead Harriers in the afternoon and still come in third or fourth. I remember one Saturday our match being called off because the pitch was frozen and I ran in the afternoon and won it. That made me realise I would prefer to do a sport where I could succeed or fail on my own merits. So I started running seriously at 16. I finished 10th in the junior cross-country championships, before I went to university. By the time I left university I was the world's worst runner. I didn't realise at the time but I was anaemic and the more I ran the worse I got. So I started taking iron tablets and never looked back.

I came back to teach chemistry at St Joseph's from 1970-74 and that's when I started running for Great Britain. My training consisted of running five miles to work every morning then ten miles – the long way home – every night. I remember breaking the two-mile world record in 1973 and when I came back to school on the Monday morning that's all the kids wanted to talk about. So I had to shut them up! It was also great to break the 3,000 metres world record in 1974 on home turf at the Gateshead International Stadium.

From the age of seven or eight it would be day trips to South Shields, which has remained a favourite place of mine, not least because the Great North Run finishing line looks on to the beach there. And in 2014 we will have had one million finishers across the line – the first mass sporting event to reach that milestone. So it's fantastic to see how it has become the UK's biggest road race since I launched it in 1981. My wife Sue and I love that whole Northumberland coastline around Embleton looking to Dunstanburgh Castle. We've been there in the depths of winter when it's just the two of us and when it's packed with sunbathers in summer. So we've experienced the hottest and coldest days there and it's always glorious. It's particularly special when the huge flocks of Arctic terns come in the spring. We love all the great walking around there from Budle Bay and Ross Sands to Holy Island.

The Great North Run is the UK's biggest road race

"I love that whole Northumberland coastline around Embleton looking to Dunstanburgh Castle. It's particularly special when the huge flocks of Arctic terns come in the spring."

ROBSON GREEN

actor and TV presenter

Robson Green first made his name in the BBC drama Casualty *but has starred in a string of television dramas in a 30-year career including* Soldier Soldier, Grafters, Waterloo Road *and* Wire in the Blood, *which was made by his own North East TV production company Coastal Productions. He also presents* Extreme Fishing *on Channel 5.*

I'VE SPENT MOST OF MY CAREER away from Northumberland but it's what brings you back. It's been my hinterland, my upbringing and socialisation. It's my sense of self, identity, family and belonging. That's why I love this place. It's who I am. I'm the son of a miner and my father and his fathers before him were decent, hard-working, honest men. The pits crafted a certain sort of person and the coal-mining industry fuelled the industrial revolution and powered the workshop of the world. My dad was very left of centre. I've inherited his political outlook and his love of Newcastle United football team.

My family were all from Hexham and Rothbury. I'm not a city dweller although I love the fine architecture of Newcastle and the fantastic bridges across the Tyne. My father always took me to the countryside as a boy. His passion was coldwater swimming so we would go to Alnmouth, Seahouses and Druridge Bay. I love Bamburgh beach – that's where Mum and Dad were at their happiest, just walking along the sand. I think it comes from working underground, that need to get out in the fresh air. Dad had a little Hillman Imp. It was his pride and joy and it took us everywhere. It might take us two or three hours to get to Seahouses. It didn't matter. His brother was a fisherman and he took me to the River Coquet at the age of seven. He tied me a fly and taught me fly fishing. I saw a kingfisher. I caught a trout and we ate it. The die was set but I never imagined that marvellous first experience would end up taking me to where it has.

I've worked in over 100 countries, fished as far afield as New Zealand and Peru and I've spent long periods away from home in places like Australia and South Africa. But I was born near Dilston Hall in Hexham and I'm back there again now. I'm just like the salmon that travels vast distances but returns to the very spot where it was born.

© Gary Walsh

I grew up in Dudley in North Tyneside – where my dad worked down the pit – and went to school there. I don't know where the acting gene came from, although my parents were great fans of the cinema and theatre. I do remember inspirational teachers like Howard Beckett, who is still teaching music and drama and Mrs Moffit and Mrs Mackenzie who taught me English. I had no desire to go down the pit and was lucky enough to be born at a time when there were other possibilities for youngsters. After school I joined Swan Hunter at 16 as

"I'm just like the salmon that travels vast distances but returns to the very spot where it was born."

The beautiful Coquet valley

an apprentice draughtsman. But in my spare time I was at Backworth Drama Centre three times a week. Live Theatre director Max Roberts gave me my first big break and took a big risk on a lad who hadn't been to drama school and with no theatrical background. He told me I had what it takes to survive in this world of acting – and if you can make a living out of it that's a bonus. I really don't think I have surpassed the work I did with the Live Theatre in the early days. I was working with material from terrific writers like Tom Hadaway, Alan Plater, Lee Hall and Peter Flannery. My first ever professional job at the Live directed by Max Roberts was a Tom Hadaway play called *The Long Line* – one of my favourites – and I met Kathryn Tickell for the first time. She played the Northumbrian pipes throughout and that sound gives you an instant emotional connection and sense of place and peace.

Alongside the acting I was always singing as a youngster too. We formed this band called The Workie Tickets – after one of my dad's favourite expressions. It was an 'a capella' band and we would do all those old Phil Spector wall-of-sound type harmony songs like *Da Doo Ron Ron* by The Crystals and *Be My Baby* by The Ronettes. Our final gig was at the Royal Albert Hall in front of 7,000 people and I thought that was a good place to stop.

Because I travel all over the world for my work it's great to come home. People are so busy these days and under so much pressure. Northumberland takes me away from all the stress. People there are at ease with themselves. For me it's like a Blue Zone – those geographic areas where people's life expectancy is higher than anywhere else, as described in Dan Buettner's book. I love the Coquet Valley. One of my favourite spots is the little village of Thropton when you turn the corner from Rothbury and there are glorious views across the valley to the Simonside hills beyond. I lived there for 14 years in a house that overlooked the valley and had two miles of fishing rights on the river. My home now is back in Hexham right on the banks of the South Tyne. Again, the stunning views and the birdsong. What could be better for your soul?

www.**robsongreen**.com

"It's my sense of self, identity, family and belonging. That's why I love this place. It's who I am."

JILL HALFPENNY

actress and dancer

Best known for her TV roles in Coronation Street *and* EastEnders, *Jill Halfpenny's career began with* Byker Grove. *She has also appeared in* Waterloo Road *and* Wild at Heart. *In 2004 she won* Strictly Come Dancing. *On stage she has played leading parts in* Chicago, Calendar Girls *and* Legally Blonde.

AS A KID I WAS LIKE A SPONGE. I used to watch the older children on our estate in Leam Lane, Gateshead – whether it was playing cricket on the street, acting out games, staging mini-Olympics – and I would drink it all in. I was in awe of it all and loved being part of a group. Going into performing and joining a cast was a natural progression, I suppose.

I went to dancing school not far from where I lived and all I wanted to do was be in shows or just get involved and be part of something. There would be adverts for children to take part in productions and I would always apply. At the age of nine or ten I got lucky when I got a part in *Sweeney Todd* at the Newcastle Playhouse, as it was called. Having a chaperone, joining rehearsals and being on stage was wonderful, and I knew then that this was exactly what I wanted to do.

I wasn't necessarily the best singer in the drama group or the best dancer but I was constantly watching and listening. They say you have to be exceptional to stand out, to really make it in some walks of life, but at that time I was mostly just taking it all in and learning everything I could.

I remember saying to my mam how great it would be if there was a Geordie version of *Grange Hill* – then *Byker Grove* came along! Starting in that show at the age of 13 was like a fairytale for me. I was just buzzing and loving every minute, and the show was drawing a lot of attention. It's funny after all the things I've done since that it's still what a lot of people remember.

The thing I'm proudest of, when I look back, is that I never questioned whether I could move into that kind of world. I never thought that council estate people like

Jill in Strictly Come Dancing *on tour at the Metro Arena*

"I stand outside the theatre, looking up the sweep of Westgate Road with its bike shops and grittiness."

Jill in Inspector George Gently *with Lee Ingleby and Martin Shaw*

me didn't get to do things like that – I just wanted to do it and I did. It's probably the way I was brought up: no one really pushed me but no one held me back either. I got a lot of encouragement but it was me who pushed myself. There were a few times when I could have been scared off but I had a one-track mind and just kept going back.

Having the freedom I had as a youngster probably helped too. There was a lot of green around our estate so there was plenty of space to run around, join in with loads of other kids and just play for days on end. I couldn't give my son Harvey that amount of freedom where we live in London.

When Harvey was born we moved back to the North East near Stocksfield for a while, but went back to London because it was just easier with work. But I still desperately yearn to be round my family and I love going home. So does Harvey. His dad and I are both Geordies and he's even got a bit of a Geordie accent. He knows he sort of belongs there, too.

As a child I'd go on day trips to the coast – Whitley Bay, Cullercoats, Spanish City – but nothing had the magic for me of Westgate Road in Newcastle where the Tyne Theatre is. That's where I spent years and years of my life rehearsing and performing, being in pantos. It's my second home and I adore it. I still get the same feeling when I go back there and stand outside the theatre, looking up the sweep of Westgate Road with its bike shops and grittiness. It's not so much about what you see but more about the way it makes you feel.

"Nothing has the magic for me of Westgate Road in Newcastle where the Tyne Theatre is. That's where I spent years and years of my life rehearsing and performing. It's my second home and I adore it."

LEE HALL

writer

Lee Hall found fame with the 1999 hit movie Billy Elliot *and adapted it for the stage in 2005, winning an award for best new musical. His award-winning play* The Pitmen Painters *premiered at the Live Theatre in Newcastle and later went on to Broadway.*

I WENT TO BENFIELD SCHOOL in Walkergate, east of Newcastle, and sixth form college in Tynemouth. I was very lucky to have inspirational teachers. At Benfield it was Chris Heckles. She was very influential and really got me into drama. I didn't really go to the theatre as a kid. It wasn't something we did in our family but I started writing, acting and making things up at school long before I was a regular theatre-goer. That was one of the gifts she gave us. It wasn't high culture or art, just something you had fun doing.

My family were actually very supportive. They just thought I was weird and wondered why I was interested in this stuff! At school, though, it was a hard, working-class place. There was a lot of incomprehension and distrust and you got picked on. I liked music and played violin and guitar and you got bullied for it. But in a way it made you stronger. I thought: "I'm going to fight to do my art." It made me challenge myself about what I wanted to do and why it was important.

It's always been my mission to write something those guys could understand. It doesn't have to be arty-farty or airy-fairy and above people's heads to be intelligent and emotional and relevant. And drama shouldn't talk down to anyone. Although it's about art, *The Pitmen Painters* is a comedy as much as anything. You can probe the issues about art and class but you can enjoy it as a good laugh and a good night out. I see *The Pitmen Painters* as a prequel to *Billy Elliot* in some ways because it's set 40 years before. They are like Billy's granddad. Like *Billy Elliot* it's an uplifting and moving play, but it's also very funny. We're in love with the subject and the characters because it's a true story and it's part of our heritage.

Tom Holland plays Billy Elliot in the stage production

It's very important to me coming back to Newcastle and paying my dues, as it were. In the cast of *The Pitmen Painters*, for example, there are people I went to school with and people I went to sixth form with and most of the rest I know from my youth theatre days. The Live Theatre was very important in my early development. There's a whole community of us – actors, writers and directors – who grew up at the same time and we share the same view of theatre: it should be popular and fun.

It's so rare for a writer to be able to work with a pool of acting talent that you know so well. They understand you and play it in the way you've imagined it. Chris Connel (the main character Oliver Kilbourn in *The Pitmen Painters*) was at school with me, and Ian Kelly (the posh teacher Robert Lyon) is a friend of mine from Cambridge University.

Although I live in London I always think of Newcastle as my home, especially emotionally. I never feel like I've entirely left. My mum still lives in Newcastle so I come back quite a bit to see her and I still do a lot with

"Although I live in London I always think of Newcastle as my home, especially emotionally. I never feel like I've entirely left."

The Lit and Phil Library

The Pitmen Painters *premiered at Newcastle's Live Theatre*

The Crown Posada pub in Newcastle

the Live. It's a tremendous resource and I'm very proud to be associated with it.

I love Newcastle and I've always written about it. It's somewhere that is very distinctive and it stays with you. It's a very dramatic place to come back to – situated on the river with all the bridges. You can slip quietly into a place like Manchester through the suburbs, but arriving back in Newcastle is always a dramatic experience – crossing the river on the Tyne Bridge and St James' Park dominates the skyline.

My two favourite rooms in Newcastle are the Crown Posada and the Lit and Phil. I love them both very much. My favourite view is from the Free Trade pub looking up the River Tyne towards the city. It's stunning.

The architecture and history are important in the North East but it's the character of the people that I hope I celebrate most in my work. Even if the characters are flawed and difficult they have a tremendous spirit, which you can't help but celebrate.

"My favourite view is from the Free Trade pub looking up the River Tyne towards the city. It's stunning."

BRENDAN HEALY

actor, musician and comedian

Brendan Healy started his professional life as a musician but has since enjoyed a 40-year career as an actor, theatre writer and producer – and more recently as a comedian. He has appeared in TV dramas including Auf Wiedersehen, Pet *and* Spender *and is a regular performer at the biennial Sunday for Sammy concerts at Newcastle City Hall.*

I WASN'T REALLY CUT OUT FOR TELEVISION. I got my first job on the Tyne Tees TV kids' show *Razzmatazz* in the Seventies but I used to speak my mind and say things were bollocks – which is not great when you are on television! But let me take you back a bit. I was posh and grew up in Jesmond. I went to St Cuthbert's Grammar School in Newcastle along with Sting, Ray Laidlaw from Lindisfarne and Neil Tennant from the Pet Shop Boys. I say went – I just popped in occasionally, really. And that was the problem because it was an academic school. And we were a Catholic family. My dad had been there and my uncles had been there and there was this expectation from the priests who ran it. So if I did anything wrong I got it twice: once from the school and then again when I got home. When I left I remember running into an old teacher who was as tough as old boots and used to batter us, the old bugger. I told him I had just finished music college and was about to work in a theatre company. He told me he always thought I'd do well. I said: "Then why did you batter me?" So through adversity I ended up in showbusiness. Maybe battering is not such a bad thing! I've worked solidly for 40 years. I've never been rich or famous but I've brought up a family of four kids and paid all my bills and made a living out of it.

I lived in London for a while but I couldn't wait to come home. It would have been easier for me to live there for work. But this is me. I am the North East. I love the countryside, the seaside and Newcastle. I live in Haydon Bridge and I love the village and sense of identity where everybody knows you – like the postman, the landlord, the butcher and unfortunately the policeman! But I love coming into Newcastle too because I really appreciate what a fabulous city it is with the Grainger Market and old Eldon Square and the terrific buildings. Now that I've moved to the Tyne Valley I seem to appreciate it more. The North East has got everything that you'd want. I love the Northumberland coast too and especially Bamburgh in the winter – windsurfing in the North Sea looking at the castle with that cold but bright winter light and the Farne Islands behind you.

When I was a kid we would go to Holy Island every Whit and stay at Mrs Luke's guesthouse. My uncle Brian would stay at the only other guesthouse on the island and we would be the only tourists there. It was magical, mysterious and mystical. Being locked on a tidal island when you are a kid – it's Famous Five stuff. The sense of adventure. You could go out to play and you could go absolutely anywhere you wanted and you were completely safe. It's a very special place.

People sometimes say to me: "Brendan, how do you describe the North East to people who don't know it?" I say: "Well, take Bamburgh beach on a beautiful sunny day. You have a stunning medieval castle, originally home to the kings of Northumbria, watching over you. You are gazing at the Farne Islands, which symbolises one of the greatest acts of heroism the planet ever produced in Grace Darling. It also just happens to be one of the best bird and seal sanctuaries in the world. It is a world-designated Area of Outstanding Natural Beauty. Just there is a tidal stream running down to the beach and next to that are Elysian rock pools where you can swim without a soul to bother you. And you want me to tell complete strangers about it so they can come and ruin it. You must be joking!"

Brendan loves clowning around on stage

Sir Bobby Robson was a very special man and it was an honour to perform at the Sage concert to celebrate what would have been his 80th birthday in February 2013. They called him a 'beacon of humanity' at the tribute and that says it all about him.

People often joked that he couldn't remember names. Everyone has their own view on it. My view was he'd met millions of people in his life – how could he be expected to remember every name he ever met? I thought he didn't know my name but I was proved wrong when I did an after-dinner speech at St James' Park to mark a Fairs Cup anniversary. The place was full of football bigwigs. I suddenly froze. I didn't know anyone at the do and I don't know anything about football anyway. Suddenly Bobby caught my eye and at the top of his voice shouted: "All right Brendan, son?" What a lovely thing to do to put me at my ease and help me through it. What a generosity of spirit. What a lovely fella.

www.brendanhealy.co.uk

"I love the Northumberland coast – especially Bamburgh in the winter."

TIM HEALY

actor

Tim Healy is best known for playing brickie Dennis Patterson in the Eighties television drama Auf Wiedersehen, Pet *and as Lesley the transvestite in the ITV comedy* Benidorm *but he has also enjoyed a glittering career on stage and in film for more than 30 years.*

MY EARLIEST MEMORIES are of Benwell. My mam and dad had a little shop and we lived in the flat upstairs with an outside loo. We'd play football in the streets – a game of doors with two doors on one side of the street, one goal and two doors on the other one. My uncle Bob lived on the other side of Elswick Road and I used to go over to see him on a home-made skateboard fashioned from an old Eagle annual and a roller-skate.

We moved to Birtley when I was nine and it seemed like the middle of the countryside. I'd never seen fields and cows before. My dad got a job at the Royal Ordnance Factory and bought a little modern Leech house. We were so chuffed to have a proper house with an upstairs and downstairs. We were one of the first families in the street to get a car too – we had a little Morris Minor, which took us everywhere.

My dad was a very keen amateur actor and I loved to help out by putting the spotlight on him or doing the curtain. When I was 11 my first-ever part was with my dad in *Finian's Rainbow*. I was given the role of Henry, a little black boy. I insisted on doing my own make-up. But I forgot to do the legs. So I went on stage with a black face and white legs! But I fell in love with the whole thing.

I remember when I was a little lad – when they still had the trolley buses – going to the Quayside market. It was a North East institution – everyone went there at the weekend. In particular I remember this little old Pakistani fella who used to sell duvets on his stall and he had this brilliant Geordie patter just like Bobby Thompson.

People used to turn up from far and wide just to listen to him. He was hilarious.

Tim, left, with the rest of the Auf Wiedersehen, Pet *gang*

I left school and got an apprenticeship at the Caterpillar factory. It was seen as the thing to do. The construction industry was booming in the Sixties. But I hated every minute of it. As soon as I finished serving my time as a welder I threw the tools down. I found out about a drama course at Durham Tech and started doing my A-levels. The problem was I couldn't get a grant to pay for it so I had to make some money.

I saw this ad in the Evening Chronicle: "Court jester wanted". So I rang them up. They asked me whether I could sing and crack a couple of gags. I told them no problem, so I got the job. It was at Langley Castle and I

"Hartside is stunning and it changes dramatically with the seasons. In the autumn it's all amber and red and in the winter you've got the snow banked up on the sides. It's almost like being on a toboggan run."

Newcastle Quayside market

was working seven nights a week. I bought a little Riley car and it would take me an hour and a half to get there. But at least that got me an Equity card. You needed one in those days. Another ad in the paper got me an audition for the newly established Live Theatre on Newcastle's Quayside. Jimmy Nail's sister Val McLane and Kevin Whately's wife Madelaine Newton were already there.

We started by rehearsing on the 13th floor of a block of flats in Gateshead. We got a small grant from Northern Arts but we couldn't afford a van in those days so we bought this old ambulance. We used to turn up in this battered old thing for gigs at workingmen's clubs. We'd get some very funny looks. We got Geordie author Tom Hadaway on board as a resident writer and never looked back. Tom wrote my first TV show: a 1970 BBC Play for Today called *The Happy Hunting Ground.* Tom wrote his stories about the fish quay in North Shields but they were universal stories about the world – they just happened to be set there. He was a brilliant writer.

That start got me a part in *Coronation Street*, then *World Cup: A Captain's Tale* then *Auf Wiedersehen, Pet* and that changed my life. By the fourth episode it was getting 17 million viewers. I couldn't walk down the street any more. I went into Marks and Spencer in Newcastle to buy some underpants and I was there for over an hour. I think I must have been introduced to everybody who worked there. But I can't grumble. I've worked most of my life and I still get excited about going to work.

Now, 30 years on, the Live has got a Lottery grant and we have a wonderful facility in Newcastle. It's the love of my life and we've got a brilliant breeding ground for talent in the North East. I directed Robson Green in his first-ever show there as a 16-year-old lad and lots of good actors have come through the ranks. I feel so proud when I go there and I've got my name on the back of my seat like some big Hollywood director.

It's a wonderful feeling being home. Since 1988 I've had a house in High Mickley in the Tyne Valley – or God's allotment as I call it. It looks right across the Cheviots. I love the view if you are driving back across from the Lakes over Hartside top down into Haydon Bridge, Alston and Whitfield. The countryside is stunning and it changes dramatically with the seasons. In the autumn it's all amber and red and in the winter you've got the snow banked up on the sides. It's almost like being on a toboggan run.

"Since 1988 I've had a house in High Mickley in the Tyne Valley – or God's allotment as I call it. It looks right across the Cheviots."

MELANIE HILL

actress

A RADA graduate, Melanie is best known for television roles in Bread, Auf Wiedersehen, Pet, United *(in which she played the mother of North East football heroes Bobby and Jack Charlton) and* Waterloo Road. *She also starred in the film* Brassed Off *and acts regularly on stage.*

I GET MORE AND MORE NOSTALGIC about the North East as time goes on and I often think about moving home. These days I really appreciate where I come from. It's a different feeling from when I was young and ambitious and chasing the bright lights. The one regret I have is that my kids, who were raised in London, don't really have that emotional tie to the region – to them it's just somewhere they visit from time to time. When we go up together I always well up when we see the Angel of the North. My girls look at me and say "what's the matter with you?" – it's a bit gutting!

I was raised in Fulwell, Sunderland where I lived with my gran and granddad, and I went to Monkwearmouth School. The place that has the best memories for me is the Cat and Dog Steps at Seaburn. They're really steep steps that take you down to a lovely sheltered bay where I used to build sandcastles as a kid. Whenever I'm back in the area I go there with my partner Jimmy whatever the weather is like, wearing balaclavas and hats and gloves if we have to, and we sit on the beach having a bacon sandwich and enjoying the sea. I think it's the most beautiful spot on the planet.

Another place I get really nostalgic about is Weardale. We used to go on day trips there with my parents in our old orange Ford Escort. My dad, probably because of being in the Army, used to try to teach us to survive in the wild. We'd have a packed lunch and a windbreaker and just enjoy the landscape. He even used to make us bury our poo so we didn't have any effect on the environment! We'd drive around by little streams on little country roads, then get stuck and have to reverse back

St Andrew's Church, Seaburn where Melanie was confirmed

"The place that has the best memories for me is the Cat and Dog Steps at Seaburn. They're really steep steps that take you down to a lovely sheltered bay where I used to build sandcastles as a kid."

Melanie with Kevin Whately in Joe Maddison's War

and my mum and dad would be arguing. In my mind I've got this lovely memory like a yellowing photograph and I've been back there driving around and trying to find that same scene, but I've never found it.

My mum's from Sunderland and she got married at St Andrew's Church in Seaburn. That's also where I was confirmed. It seemed to be absolutely massive when I was a kid and I remember there was a huge church choir then. I'm a friend of the church and I love it.

One of my favourite memories of my mum is on the day that Sunderland won the FA Cup in 1973. She went to the match and I remember her tottering about – she'd had a few – in a red-and-white mac and scarf carrying a plastic FA Cup!

I've been a lifelong Sunderland supporter and still go when I can. I've got a group of friends who are absolutely fanatical who never miss a game. When I was a teenager at Roker Park the atmosphere was just fantastic with everybody swaying around and literally sweeping you off your feet. We'd stand in an area called 'the cage' where everyone went mental and would chuck themselves around. I wouldn't fancy that much now. The new Stadium of Light is great and it's still got a great atmosphere. I think our fans are among the best supporters there are.

A defining point in my life was when I was 16 and got chosen to be in *Alright Now* for Tyne Tees Television which was a sort of forerunner for *The Tube* with live music from bands. A group of us were called the Coffee Bar Kids and we would interview the stars like Ian Dury and The Police. There were established acts and up-and-coming local bands like The Toy Dolls and Showbiz Kids. I still keep in touch with some of them. Those were great times, being on the TV and going to nightclubs like Julie's in Newcastle and Annabel's in Sunderland.

That's where I really got a taste for performing, I suppose. One of the things I'm proudest of is being in *Auf Wiedersehen, Pet*. I played Hazel in the second season of the show. It was massive and special for me: pure gold. Something like that with untested actors like Jimmy Nail wouldn't get made now: you'd have to have ex-soap actors under the age of 24. I also loved being in the film *Brassed Off* with Stephen Tompkinson who's originally from Stockton. I'm very proud of that film and the ethos behind it, supporting miners.

More recently I've spent a bit of time working at the Live Theatre in Newcastle – it's the best theatre ever, with the audience in a cabaret-seating set-up. I love it. It's a place where new writers and young people get a chance. It's by the Quayside, which is a fantastic area now, and the views of the river are wonderful. If we were to move back to the region, I'd be really torn between Sunderland and Newcastle.

"In my mind I've got this lovely memory like a yellowing photograph of Weardale with little streams and country roads."

STEPH HOUGHTON

footballer

In the 2012 London Olympics Steph was the leading goal-scorer for the GB ladies football team, netting the winning goals against New Zealand and Brazil. She is also captain of Arsenal Ladies and lifted the FA Women's Cup for the team in 2013. She previously played for Sunderland and Leeds.

FOOTBALL WAS MY FIRST LOVE. All of my family are very sporty and my dad used to play semi-professional football in Northern League sides. That's where I got my love for the sport from. There was nothing better after finishing school than spending every spare minute kicking a ball around.

I wasn't the only girl. My cousin Amy used to play as well and the lads were always happy for us to get involved. When I think back to being a child the main thing that comes to mind is always playing football, either in the schoolyard, in the streets or South Hetton cricket club near my home. That was my world.

It never occurred to me as being strange at all, being a girl and being so mad on football. Some of the parents at my school were maybe doubting why I was playing, but there was no question about how much I loved it or how dedicated I was to the sport.

My parents James and Amanda were behind me all the way. They encouraged me to be serious about football and to take it as far as I could, but they also kept me grounded off the pitch. They knew when I first started that, even if I made it, it wouldn't necessarily be my job forever so they made sure I got an education. I went to sixth form college in Durham and afterwards to Loughborough University.

Outside football I was just the same as any other girl, going shopping with my friends in Sunderland or to the Metro Centre and going to concerts. And I have happy memories of going to the beach at South Shields and going for the day to Hamsterley Forest with the whole family on our bikes.

I first played professionally for Sunderland – that's where I learned my trade. I was a Sunderland supporter and that will always be my favourite club. I grew up there, both as a person and a player, and I will always love that club and want the best for them. I learned so much there with a great coach, Mick Mulhern. He has done wonders at Sunderland and is a real inspiration.

Unfortunately, when I was 18, we were relegated. I wanted to carry on playing in the best league so I moved to play for Leeds. I was there for three years but I had a series of injuries so it wasn't a great time for me because of that. But injuries are part and parcel of the sport and, in the end, I am a stronger and fitter player as a result.

Then Arsenal came in for me and it was the best decision I have made to go to that club. It's brilliant and so professional. It was such a proud moment for me as captain when we won the FA Women's Cup.

An equally proud moment was with Team GB in the Olympics in 2012. I scored the only goal against Brazil at Wembley in front of 70,000 people. That was pretty special.

My career is obviously massively important to me, and moving away from home was never an issue but when you're away from the region and then go back to visit you realise what a special place it is. The people here have such a passion for life – and especially football. For me, the North East is all about football and I'm happy that I'm part of it.

"I was a Sunderland supporter and that will always be my favourite club."

"I have happy memories of going for the day to Hamsterley Forest with the whole family on our bikes."

RAY JACKSON

musician and artist

Ray 'Jacka' Jackson was joint lead vocalist, mandolin and harmonica player with North East folk-rock group Lindisfarne from 1970-1990. He now lives in Bampton, Oxfordshire with his wife Sandie where he has an art studio.

I WAS BROUGHT UP in Wallsend, at 42 Hunter Street, named after Swan Hunter shipyard. Sting's dad used to deliver our milk. I remember as a kid huge ships being built on the Tyne at the bottom of our street that dwarfed the terraced houses. I still have a painting of my street – featuring the Shell oil tanker Ottawa – which I did when I started art school. Stone sets on the cobbled streets marked where the Roman Wall was.

My father worked for Wallsend Co-op as a butcher for a while and he changed jobs a few times. He was a saw doctor at Wallsend Slipway & Engineering Co. and ended up as a cigarette machine operator at WD & HO Wills on the Coast Road before he retired. My mother worked at Reyrolles in Hebburn – they supplied switch gear and transformers to the power industry.

I went to Carville Junior School and Western Secondary Modern in Wallsend then later to the Newcastle College of Art and Industrial Design. The buildings are long gone. Everywhere I ever lived or was educated as a kid has been pulled down. I have got no heritage left – nowhere to show my kids. But interestingly enough Hunter Street is now the site of the Roman camp Segedunum museum.

All the streets had fantastic communities back in the Sixties. Then in the Seventies they were all displaced into modern housing estates with no soul. It's very sad my first home has gone.

We would have street trips away in the summer to places like Newbiggin-by-the-Sea. It was exactly like being at home. The men would go to the pubs and the women would sit outside with the kids chatting and knitting. We'd paddle in the freezing cold North Sea.

Lindisfarne at Newcastle City Hall

I was an only child and we were always outside playing football or messing about down on the river. There was a gambling ring there where blokes used to toss coins. There was always a look-out in case the police came, because it was illegal. It was in the days before betting shops.

I was 11 when I started playing the harmonica. My first harmonica was given to me by an aunt, who was a member of the WI, and she used to get me up playing Jimmy Shand and local North East songs. I won a talent show heat at Butlin's playing harmonica when I was 13. Then I saw a mandolin on TV in 1964 on Top of the Pops. It featured on a Billy J Kramer and the Dakotas song. I loved the sound and wanted one.

"It's very sad my first home has gone. I've got no heritage left. Everywhere I lived or was educated has been pulled down."

"I've played that fabulous venue more than 120 times."

My mam and dad went to Italy on holiday – they had met in Sorrento during the war – but I didn't want to go with them because I was 15 and teenagers didn't want to go on holiday with their parents. But they brought me one back. I started plonking away on it. We had an insurance man who came to the house every Saturday night to collect half a crown a week for some life assurance/insurance policy. He happened to play mandolin and gave me lessons.

We did the photoshoot for the *Fog on the Tyne* album on Holy Island in 1971. The interiors were shot at the Northumberland Arms, which I think is now a private house. The Britannia guest house is pictured on the album but we never stayed there. We visited the island quite regularly, often staying at the Lindisfarne Hotel, and rehearsed in the village hall. Although when the record came out I think some people down south thought we lived there.

It's great to see Lindisfarne gets half a million visitors a year these days. Hardly anyone went there in the early Seventies. The view from St Cuthbert's statue near the Priory over to the castle is a favourite of mine. I still love the North East and I miss the rugged Northumberland coast, the unspoilt beaches and magnificent castles. I still visit the coast most summers.

I miss a lot of the places I played as a young musician too, like the Mayfair Ballroom, the Majestic and the Club A'Gogo. I was livid when I heard the council was trying to close Newcastle City Hall, but thankfully they had a change of heart. We did those legendary Lindisfarne Christmas concerts in the Seventies when we almost lived there for a week – I've played that fabulous venue more than 120 times.

www.rayjacksonart.co.uk

"It's great to see Lindisfarne gets half a million visitors a year these days."

ALFIE JOEY

radio presenter and stand-up comedian

Alfie Joey trained as a priest before embarking on a career as a stand-up comedian. He presents BBC Radio Newcastle's breakfast show with Charlie Charlton and lives in Gateshead with wife Kati and son Charlie.

AS A DURHAM LAD one of my favourite places is Durham Cathedral, especially when they do the Lumière festival and it is all lit up. I remember going up to the top one time with my uncle when I was young and he said: "Look – from here you can see inside the prison and watch the prisoners walking around in the yard." How exciting is that as a kid? I also love the statue of Andy Capp in Hartlepool. I've always been a big fan of cartoons and his creator Reg Smythe was a North East institution. Andy Capp was like my dad in many ways – when he wasn't at work he spent a lot of time lying on the settee and going down the club!

My first home was Thornley Workingmen's Club in Peterlee. My mam and dad, Marlene and Alfred, were the stewards when I was a toddler. That was the Seventies when it was no women allowed in the bar and all quiet when the bingo was on. My dad spent most of his life down the pit but he loved club life. He didn't like working down the pit and he never wanted me to do that.

Sadly he never got to enjoy his retirement. He was made redundant from one of the last North East pits to close – Vane Tempest at Seaham – and he died shortly after. He was only in his fifties. He would have loved to see me make it as a presenter and entertainer. My story is a bit like Billy Elliot with a religious twist. Because when I was a kid I told him I wanted to go away and train to be a priest. He just couldn't get his head around it. Ironically when he died I left the religious order I was part of and finally tried my hand at showbusiness and that's what he would have loved.

I have no idea where it came from to be a priest. To this day I look back and it's like I'm looking at someone else's life. I went to a Catholic school – St Godric's in Thornley – and I had a very good headmaster, Mr Smith, who we all idolised. When the teacher says "draw in your book what you want to be when you grow up" most kids drew firemen or cowboys. I drew a Catholic priest. I went to Ushaw in Durham from 18 to 24. I wanted to go at 11 but I was persuaded to do a few years at Peterlee Comprehensive, St Bede's, first. My dad just cried his eyes out and said: "If you ever want to come home just tell me." It must have been bizarre to my parents. My mam wasn't even a Catholic.

I had a great time at Ushaw College. It was just like being at Hogwarts. That's where I fell in love with the arts and sport and my horizons were really expanded. I left Ushaw to join a religious order, the Salesians of Don Bosco, and I became Brother Alan with them for five years. It was then, at 28, that I realised my true vocation was to be an entertainer. I studied and taught drama and we had a module in stand-up comedy and I suddenly realised this is what I've always wanted to do.

I fell into radio by accident in a way. As a stand-up comic you get asked to do other things. I've had a part in the BBC3 sitcom *Ideal*. In turn doing TV threw up some radio work. It snowballed from there. The boss of Radio Newcastle wanted someone funny to present the afternoon show in 2008 then I switched to the breakfast show a year later.

I love it and every show is different because it is about the news. A lot of comedians ask me if I miss gigging, but I'm gigging every day to more than 100,000 people. It's exhilarating and draining, but brilliant. Most

© Chris Armstrong. Courtesy of Hartlepool Borough Council

people think it's about getting up early but it's actually about going to bed at 8.30pm. I don't even get to see my wife and son in this job. Anyone can set their alarm to get up early but you can't set it to go to bed early.

"I had a great time at Ushaw College. It was just like being at Hogwarts. That's where I fell in love with the arts and sport and my horizons were really expanded."

BRIAN JOHNSON

singer and lyricist

Brian Johnson has been the lead singer with rock band AC/DC since 1980 after forming the glam-rock group Geordie in the Seventies. Also a car enthusiast – his autobiography is called Rockers and Rollers *– he races vintage cars and lives in Sarasota, Florida with wife Brenda.*

I WAS ONE OF FOUR KIDS – three boys and a girl. I loved cars when I was growing up – I would spend hours sitting in my dad's first car, an old Wolseley 690 – and I loved playing football. Dunston Park seemed huge when I was a kid and looks tiny now when I go back. We'd throw down two jackets for goalposts and have a kick-about.

We couldn't really afford holidays. It would be a day trip to Cullercoats with Uncle Stan and Gran, cousin Annette, Auntie Ethel and Uncle Hughie who whistled through his teeth and Uncle Norman, who my dad said could peel an orange in his pocket with one hand. Granddad wouldn't come because he was scared his pipe would blow out.

We didn't have any money and my mam, who was from Italy, would knit us boys woollen swimming trunks. When they got wet they fell to your knees so there we were left holding our little tadgers in our hands in the freezing cold. There would be egg sandwiches and scalding hot tea. I remember my younger brother getting lost on the beach and the voice on the tannoy: "Could Mr Johnson please come and collect his son."

We would take the No. 66 Dunston circular bus to Newcastle Central Station then ride the electric train to the coast. I still remember the excitement and thrill of riding the electric train to the coast, because in those days we still had steam trains passing right behind our garden carrying coal to the power station. At night people would go and pick up the coal that fell from the trains. My dad didn't work for the Coal Board so we didn't have a pile of coal outside the back door like the

Brian, second left, with AC/DC

pitmen's families. But there was a wonderful sense of community so they would say: "Come on, Alan – our coalhouse is full. Take what you need."

When I left school at 15 I was an apprentice draughtsman at Parsons but I couldn't wait for Saturdays to come around when I could rehearse with my little band. Everyone wanted to be in a band in those days. Everyone wanted to be The Beatles or The Stones and music was your ticket out of the North East if you didn't have the brains or education.

We couldn't afford the education, but we all went to tech college on day release trying to better ourselves. Every Saturday would find me on the bus to Walker with my little 10-watt amp in one arm and microphone in the

"One of my favourite drives is up near Hadrian's Wall in Northumberland and over to the Lakes. I love driving up the Military Road, going through Fourstones and Haydon Bridge up over Hartside pass on the A686 and stop at Melmerby for a cheese scone and a cup of tea. Bliss."

other. I got the gear from Miller Music in Newcastle. It was 23 guineas for the little Watkins amp and £3 for the microphone and my dad had to sign the hire purchase agreement.

We'd practise in a little prefab house where Steve and Trevor Chance lived. Steve was our bass player and his parents allowed us to practise in his bedroom. It was the start. We'd rehearse all day then go for a beer in the evening. We were too young to get served in pubs but it was pretty loose in those days. We'd drink Guinness

Brian enjoying a pint with his dad

and cider – black velvet. It made you throw up something rotten. Then it was back on the double-decker bus to Marlborough Crescent where I'd catch the 66 circular back to Dunston. They were wonderful times – long before I formed Geordie in the early Seventies.

I live in Florida these days and I miss the North East countryside most of all. I have a grandson now so it's a joy to come back and see him. I love driving back home and seeing the magnificent Angel of the North. It always puts a smile on my face. I always think it's some guy saying: "Honestly – it's this big!"

I remember doing that drive – in the days before the Angel – for the first time with my wife Brenda, who is American. I said proudly: "There you are, my darling, that's the Team Valley." She said: "Are you sure that's not some Army barracks?" She was right!

And the shame about Newcastle these days is that, apart from Grey Street and Dean Street, I don't recognise it any more. If I try and drive through the town I end up in some no-go area with a traffic warden shouting at me. My wife calls me the 'used-to man' because every time we drive through Newcastle I say: "There used to be a pub there, or there used to be a cinema there." But I love the Crown Posada. Thank God that's still there. And the house where I was born is still there – 1 Oak Avenue in Dunston. I went back in my Ferrari and knocked on the door and asked the woman who lived there whether I could have a look inside. She just said: "Na." It didn't work out the way it would if you had a BBC TV crew with you!

One of my favourite drives is up near Hadrian's Wall in Northumberland and over to the Lakes. I love driving up the Military Road, going through Fourstones and Haydon Bridge up over Hartside Pass on the A686 and stop at Melmerby for a cheese scone and a cup of tea. Bliss.

I was working with Sting on his brilliant musical *The Last Ship* with Jimmy Nail and we were in New York walking up Fifth Avenue. Someone took a photograph of us – three Geordies on Broadway. The Newcastle circle thing doesn't end. It's there for life and we are still working together and enjoying it. When I looked at that picture of us I remember my teacher, in a posh voice, saying: "Johnson, you'll never amount to anything. It's the way you talk. If a man with half your brains talks posh he will be your boss. Get used to it." What a horrible thing to say to a kid. I'm pleased time has moved on and people are now proud of the way they talk. That's the way it should be.

I loved Sir Bobby Robson. When I finally met him at St James' Park he said: "I know you but I can't remember your name. I'm terrible with names because I meet so many people." And I'm the same. He asked me to sit and have a photograph taken with him. I thought that was magic, then he called Bobby Charlton over to join us. That picture has pride of place in my house in Florida. It gives me a warm feeling. My daughters say: "What's wrong with dad? He goes all girly when he looks at that photograph!"

Bobby's persona wrapped you in a warm blanket and everything felt good with the world.

www.acdc.com

"I love driving back home and seeing the magnificent Angel of the North. It always puts a smile on my face. I always think it's some guy saying – honestly, it's this big!"

CHRIS KAMARA

footballer and TV presenter

Chris Kamara started his footballing career at Portsmouth in 1975 after a brief spell in the Royal Navy. He played for several clubs including Stoke City, Leeds United and Sheffield United. He also managed Bradford City and Stoke before joining Sky Sports as a presenter and football analyst. He lives in Wakefield with wife Anne.

YOUR HOMETOWN IS YOUR HOMETOWN for good or bad. You always consider it to be a special place and I'm proud to come from Middlesbrough. People who look at it from afar don't see its hidden beauties. It's always been an industrial town and it always will be. You never forget that but you need to look closer and deeper, rather than just talking about the chimneys that bellow smoke and the A19.

I grew up on Park End council estate until I joined the Royal Navy at 15. We weren't very well off and struggled as a family. My dad worked for ICI and British Steel and my mum looked after me, my brother George and sister Marie. Throughout my school life – first at primary, then later St Thomas's Secondary – I was in the same class as Middlesbrough chairman Steve Gibson. We are still best friends to this day and sometimes we have to pinch ourselves to remind us what he have achieved in life.

I played school football and for 'Boro Boys. Steve never made 'Boro Boys but he did play for the school teams with me. Stewart Park in Marden, where the great Captain Cook was born, was about 20 minutes from my house and every Sunday us lads would play football there and Steve and I would go to Ayresome Park every other Saturday and watch the 'Boro. I remember we would get a 'squeeze' on the turnstiles – two youngsters would get through together for the price of one. That certainly helped my pocket money from the paper round. Stan Anderson was the manager in those days and I loved players like Eric McMordie, a stylish midfielder from Northern Ireland. Because I was a midfielder too, I tried to model myself on him.

For summer holidays we'd go to Redcar or Saltburn or Marske-by-the-Sea if we were lucky and mum and dad had saved a bit extra. It would always be them in the pub and us on the beach playing football or splashing about in the North Sea even if it was blowing a gale and freezing cold. Auntie Doreen and Uncle Dave lived over in Billingham and it was a major treat to go and see them. That meant getting the bus to North Ormesby, jumping on the Transporter Bridge then getting another bus at the other end. The Transporter Bridge is such an iconic landmark on Teesside. I always wanted to walk over the top of it. People did it in those days. I was always a bit too frightened as a kid and promised myself I would one day when I had more bottle. But I never did get round to it.

I also have fond memories of climbing up Roseberry Topping. Steve and I would get the bus to Great Ayton then walk to the top. When I later became a professional footballer at Portsmouth I would come home every summer and run up and down it for my pre-season fitness. It's a fantastic spot.

I left home at 15. My dad made my brother join the Army and me the Navy. I was only in the Navy for six months but maybe it was the best thing that ever happened to me in some ways.

A lot of the lads in the 'Boro Boys team were far better footballers than me but they all signed for Middlesbrough and none of them made it. In those days there was a big 'going out drinking' culture and footballers just weren't taught how to look after themselves. When I went to Leeds in 1990 the manager Howard Wilkinson taught us all about hydration and looking after yourself.

Chris at the races with lifelong pal and Middlesbrough chairman Steve Gibson.

In the early days it was eat what you want, drink what you want. We'd have six or seven pints after a game because that was what you did. It was really nice to come home and play a few games on loan for 'Boro towards the end of my career. That was down to Steve Gibson.

Not many people know but I almost signed for 'Boro when I was captain at Stoke and Alan Ball was the manager. Bruce Rioch was the Middlesbrough manager and I was about to sign for £150,000 but Leeds hijacked the deal. Bruce Rioch didn't take it well, but the worst thing was having to ring up Steve on the way home and tell him. Instead of celebrating a great contract with Leeds I was deflated because I'd let Steve down. Steve and I remained friends in spite of it and he got me to 'Boro to play a few games at the end of my career. So I fulfilled my ambition of playing for Middlesbrough and my dream of playing for Leeds.

My mum and dad are no longer around so the only two people I really get back to see in 'Boro are Steve Gibson and my best man Peter Connelly who still works down the docks. Every year we still have a night out in town and go to all the pubs.

"I have fond memories of climbing up Roseberry Topping. When I later became a professional footballer at Portsmouth I would come home every summer and run up and down it for my pre-season fitness. It's a fantastic spot."

SI KING

TV chef and presenter

Si King and his pal Dave Myers are the Hairy Bikers TV duo, who have fronted a host of cooking television shows with a motor-biking twist, starting with The Hairy Bikers Cookbook *in 2006 to* The Hairy Bikers Mississippi Adventures *in 2012. Si lives in the Tyne Valley with his wife and three sons.*

ALTHOUGH I TRAVEL ALL OVER THE WORLD for work I live in the Tyne Valley, and the North East is my home. This is where my moral compass is, my family, my friends and the people I love.

I have fond memories of Kibblesworth where we lived when I was little. My grandfather was a winder at the pit, my great uncle Noble was a faceworker and my uncle Ed was head of ventilation. My mam was from County Durham but my dad was from Lambeth, south London. He was bombed out in the Blitz and lost his mother in the house. He was on the Russian convoys in the Navy and came into the Tyne on a minesweeper and later he worked as a print-setter on The Journal. He was also a trained FA coach. Kibblesworth pit always had a bloody good football team. He met my mam at the Oxford in Newcastle. She was a great dancer. She told me she never danced with Americans because they had two left feet and the sophistication of an ash-pit netty! I was the youngest of three. My sister Ginny lives in Italy now and my brother William is in Australia but we've all maintained the connections with Kibblesworth.

We were also one of those families that you would see on the beach in Bamburgh in December. My dad would get us into the car. We would have a late 'cowboy breakfast' of bacon and beans from Carters, the great little butcher's shop in Bamburgh village. It would be snowing and my dad would say: "It will be all right once the wind drops."

I had a thoroughly good time at secondary school – it was St Robert's Newminster, Washington. I was a bit of a retrospective music fan so I was into bands like Ten Years After, Chicken Shack, Alvin Lee and Jimi Hendrix.

Si and Dave from their first TV series before they both lost three stones in weight

"One of my favourite North East pubs is the Boathouse in Wylam. It's not far from where I live in the Tyne Valley. It's a smashing little boozer."

"As your eyes hit land you see the most golden sand you could imagine, look up and you see Bamburgh Castle. It makes your soul sing."

I was a bit of a hippie really. My mam always said I was born 15 years too late. I was always in bands as a kid. I played drums – plenty of raw talent but no technique. But I was a big music fan. It was my raison d'être. I got my first kit at 12. It cost £102 which was a lot of money in 1979. My brother bought it for me. He had been working on an engineering contract in Saudi so he was making good money. I'd been driving my mam mad hitting saucepans in the kitchen. It was a Premier Resonator kit and it lasted me for years. I was brought up with drummers like Louie Bellson from the big band era. I loved their technique, then later it was John Bonham and Brian Downey from Thin Lizzy.

The Mayfair in Newcastle was a Mecca in my teenage years. It was a very sad day for me when it closed. It was one of those places I got drunk, stoned and laid more times than I care to mention.

Before fronting TV shows I spent 15 years working as a locations manager in the North East working on Catherine Cookson dramas. Imagine being paid for wandering around the region and picking stunning locations. It's the people that make the place but what a region to film in. Newcastle is a great city but within 20 minutes you can be in rolling countryside or on fantastic beaches. I was so proud to showcase the place I lived to the rest of the world. This is where I was born and brought up. The environment and the people have shaped me. I'm very proud to say that because I have a strong identity, accent and look. I was born with it and I will die with it.

Given my job as a location manager I could pick a dozen great places, no problem. But for me it has to be up on the Northumberland coast standing on Stag Rock taking in a 180 degree view. Look out to sea and you've got the Holy Island of Lindisfarne with all the history and spirituality that represents. As you scan the horizon you settle on the Farne Islands – so you have the Grace Darling heritage going through your head, maritime history, shipwrecks and the spirit of humanity. As your eyes hit land you see the most golden sand you could imagine, look up and you see Bamburgh Castle. It makes your soul sing. That view gives me a lump in my throat every time. It's been an inspiration for me, and a grounding for me. I feel at home. My heart and soul are at peace. There's no better place on the planet and I have been round the planet two-and-a-half-times.

www.hairybikers.com

"As you scan the horizon you settle on the Farne Islands – so you have all that Grace Darling heritage going through your head, maritime history, shipwrecks and the spirit of humanity."

MARK KNOPFLER OBE

musician, songwriter and record producer

Mark Knopfler rose to fame as the lead guitarist, songwriter and singer with Dire Straits, which he co-founded with his brother David in 1977. Since 1995 he has enjoyed a prolific solo career with seven albums and has composed film scores for movies including Local Hero. *He has also produced, recorded and toured with a string of famous musicians including Bob Dylan.*

I DIDN'T MOVE TO NEWCASTLE until I was eight – I was born in Glasgow – but we used to visit every year. Nana and my aunts and uncles were all in Newcastle because my mum was a Geordie girl. When we moved to Newcastle I went to Archibald Primary School, just off Salters Road in Gosforth. It was a great little school and my form teacher Mr English and the headmaster were both passionate about the countryside. So we did little bird projects, and went on camping trips to places like Bamburgh. With the family I would visit Druridge Bay, Craster, Alnmouth and Seahouses. That introduced me to the fabulous North East coast from a young age and it's a love that has stayed with me. My parents bought a little cottage, for about £300, up on the moors just north of Alnwick. It was a fantastic place for a kid to go at weekends. It didn't have water or electricity, so we took water from a well and used lanterns for light.

When I was little we also used to go to Cullercoats and Whitley Bay on the train from South Gosforth station and I loved the Spanish City. When you are a kid everything seems bigger. It was a magical place for me. Also the biggest fair in Europe came to Newcastle every year – the Hoppings – and it was like a magnet for me. I was always lost in the middle of it.

I got the music from my mum's brother, my uncle Kingsley, who was a boogie-woogie piano player. He had a banjo too, which I still have to this day. Sadly he is no longer with us but Auntie Winnie still is. They became real fans and she still comes to my shows – but my mum had to stop coming a few years ago because her ears couldn't take it any more.

I developed an obsession with guitars from an early

Lyrics from Tunnel of Love *on his 1980 album* Making Movies:
"From Cullercoats and Whitley Bay out to rockaway ...
And girl it looks so pretty to me just like it always did
Like the Spanish City to me when we were kids."

age. On Saturdays I used to do a circuit of all the music shops in Newcastle long before I had a guitar. I knew every inch of those shops like Windows, Kitchen's and Barratts. I was the little lad too nervous to take down a guitar. I didn't know how to play anyway and I had no money in my pockets. I remember once the desire was overpowering and I picked up a Spanish guitar in Barratts, took it down from the hook on the wall and a voice behind me said: "If you drop that, I'll drop you!"

I remember the first time I saw a Fender Stratocaster around 1960. It was in a little record shop at the bottom of Salters Road opposite the Globe Cinema and cost about £160. On the way back from school I would just stop and stare at it. I can't think how many hours I spent staring in guitar shop windows. I still do it to this day – I can't walk past a guitar shop. I wanted a Strat because of Hank Marvin and The Shadows. I still love the sound he gets on something like *Wonderful Land* – it's one of

"The biggest fair in Europe came to Newcastle every year and it was like a magnet for me. I was always lost in the middle of it. It's sad to hear that there will no more in the future. What's that about? It's part of our culture."

Mark with Dire Straits at Newcastle Mayfair in 1989 at a fundraiser for Teesside cancer victim Joanne Gillespie

Mark headlined the Sunday for Sammy concert at Newcastle City Hall in 2010

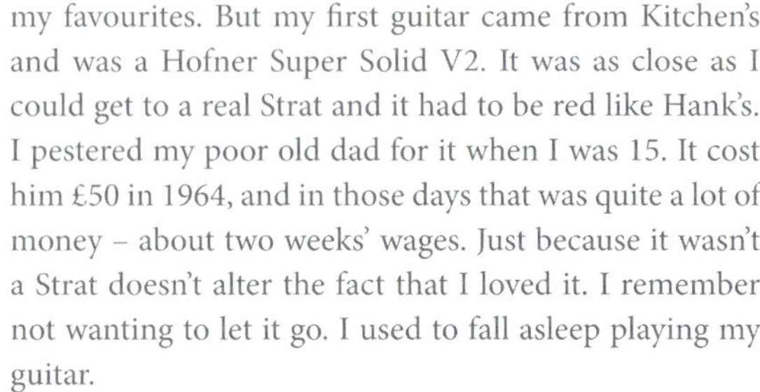

my favourites. But my first guitar came from Kitchen's and was a Hofner Super Solid V2. It was as close as I could get to a real Strat and it had to be red like Hank's. I pestered my poor old dad for it when I was 15. It cost him £50 in 1964, and in those days that was quite a lot of money – about two weeks' wages. Just because it wasn't a Strat doesn't alter the fact that I loved it. I remember not wanting to let it go. I used to fall asleep playing my guitar.

I couldn't afford an amp and I didn't have the nerve to ask my dad. I blew up the family radio by sticking a co-axial cable in the back. But it was good for me not to have an amplifier because my acoustic playing moved forward. I had a mate called Vince Harrison – he's still a mate now – and his sister Francie had her own record player. She was always bopping around to Elvis and Everly Brothers records. Later she got interested in folk music so we used to back her up and that got me into finger-picking. I started playing the folk clubs of Newcastle at 16 and I used to borrow acoustic guitars from friends. I teamed up at school with a girl called Susan Hercombe – sadly she's also no longer with us – and we played folk clubs as a duo and even got a spot on Mike Neville's BBC *Look North*.

I'd seen Chuck Berry and The Animals at Newcastle City Hall and I wanted to play electric music as well. The City Hall will always be very special for me – it seemed huge when I was 15 – so it was great to come back later and play there with my band. I also remember seeing Bob Dylan at the Odeon in 1966, which was fantastic because I was a huge fan. He played the first half acoustic then came on with his band. It was really loud and raucous. In those days before I left Newcastle to go to college I used to be a copyboy on the Evening Chronicle – on Saturday afternoons I used to get six shillings and sixpence.

When you are a teenager it's all about being in town and hanging around Newcastle but I came to realise at an early age what a fantastic county Northumberland is. I still think it's one of the best-kept secrets in the world and long may it stay that way. I don't want it to be invaded. I still fantasise about having a little cottage up in the Tyne Valley, maybe somewhere up on the tops near Allendale or Whitfield where the views are out of this world. It hasn't happened yet and it probably won't – but a man can dream.

www.markknopfler.com

"I still fantasise about having a little cottage up in the Tyne Valley, maybe somewhere up on the tops near Allendale or Whitfield where the views are out of this world. It hasn't happened yet and it probably won't – but a man can dream."

IAN LA FRENAIS OBE

writer

TV and film scriptwriter Ian La Frenais is best known for the iconic North East comedy dramas The Likely Lads *and* Auf Wiedersehen, Pet *– both co-penned with writing partner Dick Clement. Ian lives in Hollywood with his artist wife Doris Vartan.*

I GREW UP AT 3 WOODLEIGH ROAD in Whitley Bay and, although I went to Dame Allan's School in Newcastle, my teenage years were very much geared to the coast. In the summer there were busloads of Scottish girls, girls with thick Glasgow accents who chain-smoked and drank beer from the bottle. And girls from Tyneside in pencil skirts and black lipstick that chewed gum, and looked deadly. Not that I got anywhere near them, although I lived in hope.

Whitley Bay is a nice seaside town full of excitement and life in the holiday season then melancholy in the winter when it's deserted. But at that time of year, when you lived there, you owned the seafront. It was all about girls.

When I was waiting for my A-level results I worked at the Spanish City for a summer. I dreamed of being a roustabout. What could be cooler than working on the dodgems, hanging on to the pole of a moving car, managing to give change, chew gum and smoke a fag at the same time? But my dreams of being a tough guy ended there: they put me on the scenic railway where I drove infants around fairy grottos.

The Teds fascinated me most. I wanted to be a Teddy Boy so badly I got a friend's mother to narrow my drab, grey flannel school trousers to 14-inch bottoms. I loved to watch the hard guys from Wallsend or Blaydon who'd come to the coast to check each other out. It was like a fashion parade the way they would eye each other up. There were fights of course – brief skirmishes really – although I do remember a gang from Wallsend desecrated our floral clock!

BBC TV comedy The Likely Lads*: Bob glazes over as Terry puts the world to rights*

A Teddy Boy gang from North Shields befriended me for some reason. One was actually called Ted and he was a bodybuilder. His pal was Dickie, small and wiry with a Geordie accent so thick I could only understand half of what he said. They both worked at Parsons. If *The Likely Lads* is based on anyone there is probably a bit of Bob and Terry DNA in those two.

They would let me tag along to dances at ballrooms like the Plaza in Tynemouth, the Empress in Whitley Bay or the Memorial Hall in Wallsend. I recall a fight was on the cards one night and they asked whether I was with them or not. I had to say yes, of course, but I hid in the nearest lavatory I could find.

Newcastle was the big city. That was where I bought

"When you lived there you owned the seafront. It was all about girls."

"When I was waiting for my A-level results I worked at the Spanish City for a summer. I dreamed of being a roustabout."

my first records – at Windows in the Central Arcade. The ultimate Mecca of glamour was the Oxford Galleries – big bands, smoke, sweat and cheap perfume. The first live band I saw was Mick Mulligan with George Melly.

There was also a jazz club in Whitley Bay so you would get to see people like Ronnie Scott and Tubby Hayes. But the audience was all guys with beards in duffle coats and girls in black stockings – the trad jazz crowd. It was before rock'n'roll really took off although I do remember seeing Marty Wilde at the Newcastle Empire.

I don't miss the North East, as I still get back there to see cousins every year, but I have an incredible affection for it. It has been very influential and shaped me. Even now the decisions and judgments I make, and the opinions I have, are shaped by it.

I feel sad for people who lose connections with their hometown. It gives another dimension to your life.

My fondest memories as a small boy were of fantastic holidays in the Borders. I spent every Easter and most of the summer in the village of Branxton, near Coldstream at the foot of Flodden Field, where my uncle lived. He was a builder and restored beautiful old houses. He would take me around in his posh Fifties Alvis car – I can still smell the leather and walnut. He would take me to see Ford and Etal castles. There would be days in Wooler, and Cornhill-on-Tweed and up to Berwick. That's where the grown-ups would go drinking on Saturday nights, leaving me in the car with a lemonade. And after a few drinks I don't know how they drove home on those narrow, moonlit roads.

I would spend hours at the striking monument at Flodden Field (it marks the site where the famous battle was fought in 1513 between the English and the Scots) convinced the ghosts of bloodied warriors would come out of the ground and get me.

My uncle also owned and raced greyhounds and before they went off to be trained I would be allowed to exercise these beautiful animals. Those holidays gave me an enormous affection for that part of the world. When you drive up the coast and get your first view of Bamburgh Castle – what an extraordinary vista that is.

"I would spend hours at the striking monument at Flodden Field, convinced the ghosts of bloodied warriors would come out of the ground and get me."

RAY LAIDLAW

musician and producer

Drummer Ray Laidlaw is a founder member of Tyneside folk-rock band Lindisfarne who took the music world by storm with their 1971 Geordie anthem album Fog on the Tyne. *He now works as a producer with former Tyne Tees Television director Geoff Wonfor and together they masterminded the Sir Bobby Robson DVD* A Knight to Remember *and the Sir Bobby Robson 80th birthday celebration concert at the Sage Gateshead in 2013.*

AS WELL AS PRODUCING the biennial Sunday for Sammy concerts at Newcastle City Hall, it was an honour to do the *A Knight to Remember* DVD – which made £100,000 for the Sir Bobby Robson Foundation – and the Sage Gateshead concert in February 2013. It celebrated in music, song and speech, with a host of stars, what would have been Sir Bobby's 80th birthday. I was in awe of the man. He oozed charisma, and it was a privilege to film his last-ever interviews, which we used on the show.

I love the North East and I can't imagine living anywhere but Tyneside. I was born in Tynemouth and have lived there most of my life. The view from the bottom of my road Hotspur Street, next to the Grand Hotel, looking north up the coast – especially on a summer night about 10pm when it is still light – is stunning. The northern sky is glorious and you can see all the way up the coast.

I probably wouldn't have been a musician if my gran hadn't wanted me to be a priest. I was the oldest grandchild in a Catholic family so I went to St Cuthbert's Grammar School in Newcastle rather than a local school in Tynemouth. So from the age of 11, I was soaking up everything in the city. I loved The Shadows. I used to get the number 35 bus to school and it would stop outside the house in Stanhope Street where Hank Marvin lived. He was proof local lads could make it.

Some kids are into motorbikes and cars – I was into bands and all the gear. There were great music shops in Newcastle: Maxie Share's in the Grainger Market, Kitchen's in Ridley Place and Barratts on New Bridge Street – that's where the pro musicians would hang out. Teenage fashion was taking off but we got our gear from Army Surplus stores (it was fitting for the blues) and our Levis, of course, from Marcus Price.

Lindisfarne hit No 1 with *Fog on the Tyne* in 1971

I got my first drum kit in 1962. My granddad bought me a second-hand Olympic kit for ten quid, which was a lot of money in those days. I then had a second-hand Premier kit which I used for the first Lindisfarne album *Nicely Out of Tune*. After that I had a bit of money so I bought a Gretsch kit and have used them ever since.

I also formed my first band in 1962 with Simon Cowe and we played on and off for about 30 years. We were called the Aristokats and we played bingo halls and my granddad's place – the Catholic Club in North Shields. Then I was in The Druids. By 1966 I had met Rod Clements, and inspired by Chicago blues, The Beatles, Newcastle Brown Ale and Bob Dylan, we began to assemble our perfect group. Our template was local band The Junco Partners and it's brilliant to see they are still going strong. They are a North East institution.

On my CV for musical education I simply put: 'Club A'Gogo'. It was the best venue going even though it only held 300 people. That was our spiritual home and where we saw all of the big names like John Mayall's

"The view from the bottom of my road Hotspur Street, next to the Grand Hotel, in Tynemouth looking north up the coast – especially on a summer night about 10pm when it is still light – is stunning."

Downtown Faction featuring left to right Richard Squirel, Rod Clements, Ray Laidlaw and Don Whitaker

Bluesbreakers with Eric Clapton on guitar. We were called the Downtown Faction and we actually got to play the 'Gogo in September 1967. I remember standing next to Cream's brilliant drummer Ginger Baker at the bar and he ordered a quadruple vodka and orange. I thought to myself: "So that's how he does it."

In 1969 free outdoor music events were all the rage. There was Hyde Park and Golden Gate Park – why not Leazes Park? I phoned the city council and some bloke with a clipboard met me in the park the next day. I borrowed a flat-back truck for a stage and the man from the council got an electrician to take a power supply from a street lamp-post. I kid you not. No Health and Safety, no licence, no security, no problem!

About 2,000 people turned up and listened to some of Newcastle's best bands including The Callies, with Billy Mitchell, and a local singer-songwriter called Alan Hull. My band Downtown Faction went on last and we finished our set with an impromptu protest song, *Haircut Blues*. It was sung by our guitar player Si Cowe, who had been told by his employer to get his hair cut or he would be sacked. He berated his boss in song as a barber chopped off his ginger tresses on stage.

Brethren in 1969 with Ray Laidlaw at the back, Ray Jackson, Rod Clements and Si Cowe

As the Sixties drew to a close Rod, Simon and I were joined by Ray Jackson and Alan Hull. We were performing together as Brethren. Six months later we became Lindisfarne. When *Fog on the Tyne* hit number one in 1971 we were in the States. We came back famous and couldn't walk the streets of Newcastle without being mobbed.

www.lindisfarne.co.uk

Si has his ginger tresses shorn off on stage

"I love the bustle, the smells and sounds of the Grainger Market. Some of the stallholders have worked there all of their lives, it has a great community feel to it and has an atmosphere that probably hasn't changed much since it was built. I still make a detour to walk through the Grainger Market even if I don't need to buy anything. It's a magical place."

TERRY LAYBOURNE MBE

leading restaurateur

Terry Laybourne opened 21 Queen Street on Newcastle's Quayside in 1988, winning a Michelin star. It was later refurbished as Café 21, and now his award-winning 21 Hospitality Group includes Café 21, Café 21 Fenwick, Caffè Vivo and The Broad Chare, all in Newcastle, and Bistro 21 in Durham. All serve the best food from the region.

I'M NEWCASTLE-BORN-AND-BRED and, although I worked abroad for a few years, there's never been anywhere else I would call home.

I was brought up on a council estate in Lemington. It wasn't a tough upbringing at all but, when I look back, I realise money didn't flow freely. We didn't have holidays as a family – just the occasional day away – but we had fun as kids and there was always something going on. We weren't far from the river so that was always part of my landscape and we were always outside, often on our bikes. The legacy of the mining industry was on our doorstep, and the high slag heap at Lemington was both a cause of enjoyment and terror when we used to run down it as it was so steep.

I used to get up to all the usual childhood pranks like nicking apples from orchards and gooseberries from allotments – food-related stuff, funnily enough.

Having said that, I never had an ambition to be a chef. What I wanted to do was be an engineer like my dad. There were always mechanical instruments around the house and my brother, who is 11 years older than me, was a real petrol-head, so there were car parts everywhere too. At school I was good at the practical classes like technical drawing and metalwork but when I was doing my O-levels in the 1970s it was a bad time in this country with power cuts and three-day weeks and my dad said there didn't seem to be a future in heavy engineering so I should think of something else.

By chance I met a schoolmate who was an apprentice chef at the Five Bridges Hotel in Gateshead. We talked about it and he showed me some cookery books

with extravagant buffets. I got caught up in the visual aspect of it all and decided that's what I would do, so I joined him and never really looked back. It wasn't what I'd expected to do with my life, but I think of it as a form of engineering – it's just working with food instead of metal or wood.

I left home at 17 and worked in the Channel Islands, Germany and Switzerland but came home for a break a few years later – and never left.

Football plays a big part in my life: in so many areas of the city you can see St James' Park peeking out. Music, too, is important. One of my best memories of being a teenager (with long hair and platform boots, of course) is going to the Mayfair – now sadly gone – and seeing bands like The Who, Led Zeppelin, Black Sabbath and Deep Purple. It's inconceivable now that stars of that magnitude would play at such a small venue.

Newcastle itself is so special. The Tyne has always had a big place in my heart, from when I was a child playing near the river to now when I look across the Millennium Bridge in the early evening. The bridge just looms out of the ether and you can see the Sage and the Baltic rising up on the other side. World-class venues, both of them – and it's a world-class view.

www.21hospitality.co.uk

"The Tyne has always had a big place in my heart, from when I was a child playing near the river to now when I look across the Millennium Bridge in the early evening."

JOE McELDERRY

singer and songwriter

After winning The X Factor *in 2009 (with Cheryl Cole as his mentor), Joe went on to win* Popstar to Operastar *in 2011. He has a highly successful music career performing and writing songs, and was the youngest person to be awarded a Silver Heart from the Variety Club in 2013 for his charity work.*

OF ALL THE PLACES I'VE PERFORMED Bents Park in South Shields was the best. It was in 2011, I'd just won *Popstar to Operastar* and now I was going to do a show at my hometown's annual festival. It's a great event and we've had big names like Lulu and Jason Donovan before. I used to be one of the people in the audience, but this time I was on stage. I remember I was so nervous before I went on. There were 26,000 people there – it seemed like the whole of South Shields – to watch me in that park on a lovely sunny day. It was just brilliant and I'll never forget it.

South Shields has always been my home and it still is. People can't believe that it's my base with all the travelling I do, but it's only two-and-a-half hours from London. There are people at my record label who live in Kent and it takes them longer than that to get into work. Some people think the world stops at Watford Gap, but I always love coming home. I start to relax, it clears my mind and it just seems to put everything right.

I'm not complaining: my work is fantastic and I'm lucky to have the career I've got, but it's so grounding to come back and have your gran live just round the corner and the friends you've had all your life living three or four streets away. Only people who travel as much as I do would probably understand.

Nearly all my childhood memories are around South Shields. As a kid I just about lived on the beach. I'd go down there with my friends and we'd swim, light a fire, have a barbecue and wander down to where the fair is. I live only five minutes from the beach even now. I love being near the sea. When I'm away from it I'm like a caged animal. I have travelled to a lot of places with beautiful beaches but I have yet to find a coastline as unspoilt as what we have in the North East.

The beach at South Shields

The people I know from when I was younger and the support they have given me have definitely helped get me to where I am today. I was always involved in performance from about the age of 10 and I was fascinated with pantos and musicals and concerts – the lights, the costumes: it was always fascinating to me. It was like a mystical world you couldn't touch. I remember going to see Steps at the Arena in Newcastle and it was just so glamorous. But I never sang in front of anybody until I was 15. It wasn't the cool thing to do – everyone else was off playing football. It took a while to get to the point where I had the guts to sing live but I gradually built up my confidence and my friends and family were behind me every step of the way.

In the early days I sometimes did shows in pubs. Often there would be only a couple of men sitting having a pint in the back and the rest of the people in the audience would be my friends, clapping and giving support. Singing was my hobby then and I'm lucky that I've been able to make a career out of my hobby. I really don't see it as work. I know very well in this industry that your career doesn't necessarily last forever so I'm going to make the most of it and enjoy it.

I'm always determined to get better and better – I want the next album to be better than the last, the next show to be better than the one before – and I think it's that drive that keeps you going when things don't always go right. It's like a bullet train that hurtles along, knocking everything else out of the way.

www.joemcelderryofficial.com

"There were 26,000 people there – it seemed like the whole of South Shields – to watch me in that park on a lovely sunny day."

GINA McKEE

actress

Gina McKee has starred in television series including Our Friends in the North *(for which she earned the BAFTA Award for Best Actress),* Brass Eye, The Forsyte Saga *and* Hebburn. *She has had major roles in films including the blockbuster* Notting Hill *and* Wonderland. *She also appears regularly on stage.*

MY EARLIEST MEMORIES of being brought up in the North East centre around Horden, Easington and Peterlee. One of the most striking buildings in Horden is St Mary's Church. It was built in 1911, funded by Colonel Roland Burdon, and opened in 1913. We loved it when there was a wedding at St Mary's. As the newly-married couple left the church in their decorated car, the groom would throw some change out of the window for the kids. All of us would be scrambling for the pennies.

Growing up, I spent many hours in Castle Eden Dene exploring and playing. The dene is a beautiful, steep-sided wooded limestone valley. It stretches for about three-and-a-half miles from Castle Eden village, opening on to the sea at the Denemouth. High above it there's a ten-arched railway viaduct which links Horden and Blackhall. Roland Burdon and his family owned the dene from 1757 until 1951 and lived in a grand house. When I was a kid the house was forgotten and empty – and so it fuelled many stories and fantasies. I also remember the overpowering aroma of the banks of wild garlic and the abundance of wild bluebells every spring. There were red squirrels living in the dene although I only ever saw one.

Another place I loved to spend time was the beach at Crimdon. The sand dunes there are stunning, shaped by the weather and with grasses offering natural windbreaks. These sheltered hollows were a great place to enjoy a picnic. The golden sands here were such a contrast to the beaches just a few miles north which were blackened by the collieries dumping rejected coal into the sea.

St Mary's Church, Horden

"Growing up, I spent many hours in Castle Eden Dene exploring and playing. The dene is a beautiful, steep-sided wooded limestone valley."

Our Friends in the North *starring Christopher Eccleston, Gina, Mark Strong and Daniel Craig*

Gina with the cast of Hebburn*, including Vic Reeves and Chris Ramsey*

To this day, I love to visit Durham Cathedral. It never fails to fill me with awe. I think the first time I went there was on Durham Miners' Gala day. I was about four years old and still remember taking a break from dancing through the streets behind Easington Colliery's brass band and visiting the cathedral. Later at school we studied medieval history and learnt how lucky we were to have a prize example of Norman architecture right on our doorstep. Whenever I travel back on the train I look forward to that wonderful view from the viaduct as you near Durham Station. It always makes me feel happy.

In my teens I worked in Newcastle at Tyne Tees Television. I was taken aback on a recent visit to see it's gone, demolished along with The Egypt Cottage, a pub neighbouring the original building. It was probably the most unique TV station, in that, as it expanded, they simply built around the pub and sort of incorporated it! Tyne Tees had an incredibly vibrant output of programmes, most notably *The Tube*, and I met some wonderful and innovative people like Andrea Wonfor during my time there. I still hook up with Graeme Rigby, longtime member of Amber Films, and his partner Ros, from the fabulous Sage Gateshead, when I'm in Newcastle. When I was 13, they ran the Peterlee Youth Drama Workshop which is where I found out I wanted to be an actor.

"The golden sands at Crimdon were a contrast to the beaches just a few miles north which were blackened by the collieries dumping rejected coal into the sea."

CAROL MALIA

TV presenter and journalist

Carol Malia started her career as a journalist on the Hartlepool Mail at 18, before moving to Radio Cumbria. She broke into television reporting with Border TV before moving back to Tyne Tees TV in Newcastle at 24, then joined BBC North East a year later. She has been presenting Look North *since 1996.*

I WAS A TOTAL TOMBOY when I was growing up. I spent every waking hour outside in the fresh air playing. My dad was part of the Northumbria Police swim rescue team so my brother and I would always be the couple of kids in a dinghy that needed rescuing in the river at Morpeth or Hexham or in the sea at Cullercoats. I seemed to spend most of my childhood being rescued!

We lived in the Marden Estate in North Shields and there was a fire station right behind our back garden. The firemen would let us take part in their training exercises too, which was hugely exciting for us. We had great freedom as kids – a lot more than I would give my children today. I seemed to live on the edge of danger for most of my childhood and had an absolute ball.

I went everywhere on a brand new 21-speed racing bike, which was far too big for me. We'd be out playing on the building site at the top of our road or I'd cycle to my friend Sammy's house or over to Preston Grange shops. I remember that hot summer of 1976 – long days on the beach, swimming in the freezing cold North Sea and the chimes of the ice-cream van. That smell of freshly cut grass will always remind me of school exams in June.

I went to Marden High in Hartington Road. I enjoyed school but I was pretty average at everything. I was OK at netball and English and French but never really excelled in anything. At 14 I remember getting career advice from the teachers and they said I would make a good journalist because I was nosy. My dad always seemed to have a transistor radio glued to his ear walking around the house listening to the news so I suppose I was quite well informed as a teenager.

We didn't go abroad for holidays as a family. The first time I went abroad was on a ski-ing trip with the school at 13. It would be family days out to Wallington or Cragside – the same sort of thing I'm doing with my children now. We went camping a lot to the Lakes or Wales or a lodge holiday in Scotland. One year we ventured as far as Torquay, which was a big adventure.

I went to Darlington College and studied journalism after my A-levels. It was a real eye-opener being away from home as an 18-year-old for the first time. My first job was on the Hartlepool Mail and in my first week I got a front-page exclusive on a local athlete who gave me a story about not getting enough support and sponsorship from local businesses. So I wrote it up as 'Athlete blasts town's business people' and I loved the buzz of getting my first by-line story on the front page. It must have been a slow news day to be truthful but I was over the moon.

After four years on the paper I went to Radio Cumbria and that was a big transition for me. Then I got my first television job with Border TV. It was the Eighties so I appeared on screen with those big-shouldered jackets, huge earrings and massive hair! After a year I got the chance to move home to Newcastle with Tyne Tees TV at 24, which was fantastic. I had a little bachelorette place overlooking the sea in Tynemouth and enjoyed all the Newcastle nightlife. I had a ball there, then the BBC came calling and I've been there ever since, reporting at first then presenting *Look North.*

One of the great things about working in Newcastle is what you have on your doorstep in terms of fabulous countryside. I live four miles from Hadrian's Wall so I drive to work with the sun facing me as it rises and I drive home into the sun as it sets (so long as I'm not doing the late shift!) in spectacular scenery with vistas of green fields and hills all around me. It's a dream for me. I can be in Newcastle in 20 minutes or the wilds of Northumberland in 20 minutes.

I still love the walk along Tynemouth Longsands and up to the Priory because that's home for me and I never tire of it. But I adore the Simonside hills. My husband Gary and I love walking and we've hiked up Simonside countless times. When the kids are old enough they will join us too. It's a very special place for me. I took our Border collie for his first proper walk there when he was three months old. Sadly he's no longer with us but that lovely memory remains. I've been up to the top for a friend's 40th birthday and celebrated with a bottle of champagne, and I've taken friends from London up there because they are wusses and it's good for them.

In the early days of satellite TV I had a chance to go to London for a job interview but I didn't fancy it. I put selfishness before career and I have a great job here anyway. I have no regrets. Life doesn't get any better than being in the North East.

"I adore the Simonside hills. It's a very special place for me. I took our Border collie for his first proper walk there when he was three months old."

BILLY MITCHELL

musician

Billy Mitchell toured and recorded for eight years in the last Lindisfarne line-up before the group finally disbanded in 2003. He also has enjoyed a career as a solo musician and with his own group the Billy Mitchell Band.

MY DAD WORKED AT WEST WYLAM PIT and we lived in the village there until I was nine, before we moved to Newcastle then on to North Shields. I went to Prudhoe East School with Pop Robson who ended up playing football for Newcastle United. I love that area of the Tyne Valley and I still go back now and then. It's great driving out of Newcastle on the A69 and up past Heddon-on-the-Wall and looking over the valley to West Wylam and Prudhoe.

I still enjoy walking where the pit used to be and where I played as a kid. We didn't have 'soft play areas' in those days – the more dangerous it was the better. My old school is sadly no longer there, but at least it's a community centre these days.

My dad had moved to working in the office at the pit by the time it was due to close. He saw the writing on the wall and realised it was time to look around for other work. Apart from ICI there wasn't really anything else and he didn't fancy that so he started learning how to be a pub manager. My uncle had a pub in North Shields so every weekend we'd go down to North Shields so my dad could learn the trade. We eventually moved to Westgate Road to his first pub – the Mason Arms, which is long gone. I passed the 11-plus and was about to go to John Marley School in Newcastle when my dad took over the Berwick Arms in North Shields. That's still there but it's been converted into a private house now.

I've lived in Cullercoats for the past 15 years and that's got to be my favourite seaside place. I'm just one street away from the beach. It's delightful. And it's like coming full circle because we would go to Whitley Bay for family holidays when I was a kid in West Wylam. We would take the steam train from Newcastle and it was a big adventure.

I got my first guitar at ten but it was probably used more as a cricket bat than an instrument in those days. I was about 15 when I started playing seriously. My first band was called the Peasantville Dustman's Choir, which consisted of seven singers and me on guitar. We'd do numbers like *Michael Row the Boat Ashore* and *Tom Dooley*. One of the first bands I listened to as a teenager was the Kingston Trio and about two years ago I got an email from them all the way from Phoenix, Arizona. They told me they had heard my song *Born at the Right Time* and they wanted to record it and name their album after it. So it comes full circle there too.

In those early days we would play church dances but the star of the show would be a Dansette record player on which everyone played their favourite records and we would play live at the interval. Eventually we progressed to the point where we were the headline act and the record player was the support act!

There was another group in North Shields in those days called Downtown Faction with Ray Laidlaw on drums, Rod Clements on bass and Simon Cowe on guitar. They didn't have a singer so they asked me to join them. I didn't really want to join them but I enjoyed sitting in and singing the blues with them when I wasn't performing with my own band, which was doing Beatles and Hollies pop covers. So that's how I first got together with the lads who would be Lindisfarne and I ended up in the final line-up of that band from 1996 after Alan Hull died. I toured with them for eight years before the band finally split in 2003. Before that I had a great time playing and touring with Jack the Lad for five years.

Mark Knopfler with Billy Mitchell at the Sir Bobby Robson 80th birthday gig at the Sage Gateshead in 2013

It was wonderful to play at the Sir Bobby Robson Sage Gateshead gig in 2013, and a great honour. It was a bit hairy without an autocue and no time for rehearsals but it was great and the audience was fantastic. I feel lucky and privileged to do shows like that where I got to play on stage with Mark Knopfler who I have known for a long time but is also one of my musical heroes. I also enjoy performing at the Sunday for Sammy gigs every couple of years at Newcastle City Hall. They are a fantastic celebration of everything North East and I'm proud to be part of them.

www.billymitchell.co.uk

"My favourite seaside place has to be Cullercoats where I have lived for the last 15 years. I'm just one street away from the beach. It's a delightful place."

BOB MONCUR

footballer and football manager

Bob Moncur joined Newcastle United as an apprentice at 15, made his debut at 18 and went on to make 296 appearances in the black-and-white shirt. He captained the team that lifted the Fairs Cup in 1969, scoring three goals in the two-leg final, which they won 6-2. After jobs as a football manager with Plymouth, Carlisle and Hartlepool United he became a qualified RYA yachtmaster trainer with his own business. He lives with wife Camille in Low Fell.

I WAS CAPTAIN of the Scottish under-15s when I came to Newcastle for £15 a week. It was a miserable Monday morning pouring with rain when I arrived in the city on the train. Coming into the station from the North you don't get those spectacular views of the bridges. My first thought was: "What have I done here?" But as soon as I met the people I felt right at home. I made a lot of friends very quickly.

At first I was in lovely lodgings in Whitley Bay, then I got digs in Two Ball Lonnen in Newcastle's West End. I was just 18 when I met my wife Camille. She was from Lobley Hill and we met at the famous Club A'Gogo on Boxing Day. I didn't cover myself in glory on our first proper date. I took her to the pictures and fell asleep – I'd had a late night back in Scotland for the New Year!

To be honest I didn't realise how significant it was when I lifted the Fairs Cup as Newcastle skipper in 1969. I didn't really know what it meant to the fans then. But now, as the years have rolled on and I am a Newcastle supporter rather than a player, I fully realise what it meant to those great fans. I still can't believe a club of this stature has not won a cup in all those years since. I have often said the honour of being the last skipper to lift a trophy for the Magpies is an honour I would love to lose. I thought Shearer might do it and I thought the sides Kevin Keegan and Bobby Robson managed might win something but it wasn't to be. It was great to score three goals in the two-leg final against Ujpest Dozsa – all with my left foot too. People thought I was left-footed but I was actually right-footed and I worked hard on my weaker foot. It certainly paid off in those two games.

When I first went to Carlisle as manager in 1976 I wanted to sign Peter Beardsley from Wallsend Boys Club. But the board of directors wanted all the club players to live locally. I was desperate to sign him as a pro but I'd never thought about where he would live. Professionals were only on about £30 a week and lodgings cost £25 a week. So I told the board Peter would live with me. Then I had to break the news to my wife! But he was like one of the family and got on great with my son Paul and daughter Angela.

My only real ambition as a footballer was to have a roof over our heads paid for by the time I retired. When we got married we lived in a nice split-level house in Crawcrook in the Tyne Valley for about four years, then moved to a five-bed house in Darras Hall. Camille was happy to have a bigger house but it was my accountant who advised me to get a bigger mortgage for tax reasons. We've lived in Low Fell for the last 26 years. I still enjoy keeping fit and swim at Bannatyne's health club in Chester-le-Street most days.

I love the Northumberland coastline and sailing in the North Sea. I did my yachtmaster training when I was working at Plymouth as manager. Then I became a professional yachtsman and had a business for a while teaching RYA yachtmaster courses. I used to love sailing up to Amble and Alnmouth, for the weekend, anchoring in the lovely little harbour at Craster or sailing up to Holy Island, anchoring off the Priory. Then get up early and have breakfast at the Farne Isles watching the seals playing in the crystal clear waters up there. Beautiful.

I actually played against Bobby Robson when he

Skipper Bob holds aloft the Fairs Cup

played for West Brom in the early Sixties but it wasn't until the latter years that I got to know him well. I remember when he had his cancer and I was diagnosed with cancer of the colon. I've been free for more than five years now, but they had just named a suite after me at St James' Park then. Bob would come up to see me there when he was in his wheelchair towards the end. But he would never actually come inside. He would get one of the lads to come in and get me. He didn't want to come in and take the limelight away from me. He was in the last stages of his fight against cancer but his only concern was for me. That's the kind of man he was. And when he saw the plaque outside the suite with my name on it, he had a twinkle in his eye when he said: "It's good isn't it? And not before time."

"I used to love sailing up to Amble and Alnmouth for the weekend, anchoring in the lovely little harbour at Craster or sailing up to Holy Island, anchoring off the Priory. Then get up early and have breakfast at the Farne Isles watching the seals playing in the crystal clear waters up there. Beautiful."

JIM MONTGOMERY

footballer and FA Cup winner

Jim Montgomery, legendary goalkeeper for Sunderland whose double save in the 1973 FA Cup Final helped win the trophy, played more games for Sunderland than anyone else in the club's history. He went on to work with the youth teams of Sunderland and Birmingham and is now Sunderland Football Club's global ambassador.

WHATEVER ELSE I MIGHT DO in life, winning the FA Cup and – as a local lad – bringing it back to the region has got to stand out as the biggest moment. I have had some great times in football but that was unique. Nobody expected it. We were the underdogs, sixth off bottom of the Second Division. But, trained by our coaches Arthur Cox and Billy Elliott and working with our new manager Bob Stokoe, something just gelled – and look how it worked out. I can't put into words how proud we all felt, and that team still has a bond that will never be broken. Most of us still live in the region and we all got back together to celebrate the 40th anniversary of the win, sadly without Bob Stokoe and Ian Porterfield who have passed away. But we've had nothing since 1973 at Sunderland and I'd say it's long overdue.

For me, there was nothing I ever wanted do in my life except play football, and I've been blessed that I could make a living out of it. Not as much as the guys these days, though! But, just like a lot of lads from the North East, it was all I ever thought about. I was born and bred in Sunderland and as a kid I used to go to Thompson Park just past Fulwell Mill after school at St Hilda's and play football with my mates until dusk. I'd go to bed scruffy and shattered, and that's the way it was in those days. My dad used to take me to the Clock Stand in Roker Park to watch matches when I was seven or eight – great memories.

I had a wonderful childhood. I remember the house was always full of friends and neighbours and you never locked the door in those days – people would just come and go. My dad was a railway ganger down at the docks and there was never much money but we had a really happy home, with mum and dad and me and my sister Maureen. She and I both still live in Sunderland and I see her every other day.

As time went on, football became more of a possibility as a career, and I was lucky to have the encouragement and support of some great people, including my football teacher at school, Alfie Lavender, and the well-known scout Jack Hixon who got me to Burnley for a few weeks. But when the chance came up to sign for Sunderland at the age of 17 I grabbed it with both hands and never looked back.

All this time I was still playing football with my mates for fun as well as professionally. I used to go down to the Cat and Dog Stairs at Seaburn and play on the beach every Sunday morning. All the girls used to congregate there, so maybe that was part of the attraction! There were so many of us that we would play 20-a-side. If it was cold we'd get hot chocolate and if it was warm we'd get ice-cream – always from Notarianni's which was famous in the Sunderland area. I made my first-team debut just before I was 18 and still used to go down to Seaburn from time to time, but I stopped going eventually as I didn't want to get injured and land myself in trouble. I was going through a bit of a sticky time at the club then, and my manager Alan Brown – probably the best manager I played under – took me to one side and said: "You know, Jim, you've never been the same since you stopped playing on the sands." I never knew he used to watch those games. Anyway, my form picked up and all was well again. I also used to play cricket in the summer for Wearmouth Colliery to keep fit. You wouldn't see that happening these days.

Jim celebrates with Bob Stokoe

When I look back, my world was quite small then. We didn't have day trips or family holidays or anything like that, and the farthest away I got was a school trip to Chester-le-Street, swinging on a rope over the river. The rest of the time I'd be playing football locally, jumping over people's fences and running across private fields to get to the nearest convenient spot to kick a ball around. Obviously that changed and I've done my fair share of travelling – and as the club's global ambassador, I travel for work regularly to places including Malta and Korea – but it's always good to get home. There are some great places in the world and in the North East but, for me, there is nowhere like Seaburn.

www.safc.com

"I made my first-team debut just before I was 18 but still used to go down to the Cat and Dog Stairs at Seaburn and play on the beach every Sunday morning."

JIMMY NAIL

actor, musician and writer

Jimmy Nail rose to TV fame playing brickie Oz in the ITV drama Auf Wiedersehen, Pet *in 1983. He has since carved out a 30-year career as an actor, musician, film producer and television writer. In 2000, with Tim Healy, he set up the Sammy Johnson Memorial Fund to help develop young artistic talent in the North East.*

I ORIGINALLY LEFT NEWCASTLE for London in 1973 so it's been 40 years now. My sons were born and grew up in London so that's where I think of as home. But Newcastle is where I was born. I'm proud to be known as a Geordie and I'll always support NUFC.

I was first introduced to Sir Bobby by then-chairman, Freddie Shepherd – taken into the manager's office, if you please – and we had a right old laugh over a cup of tea and a biscuit. He told me how much he'd enjoyed watching *Auf Wiedersehen, Pet*, which was great to hear. Meeting Sir Bobby was a big thing for me. It was great to be with another grown-up who was as black-and-white daft as I was (and still am). I would meet him again over the years, always courteous and polite to a fault – he was a very special person. It's a safe bet there'll never be another England manager who can include miner on his CV.

St James' Park, in all its guises past and present, has figured large throughout my life: as a kid I would stand among the thousands of cloth-capped men crammed into the Leazes End, all of us cheering our beloved Magpies on. It made absolutely no difference a lot of the time, but we kept at it. It's made a guest appearance in just about every TV series I've made. The sheer size and scale of the place – situated as it is right in the middle of the city – still has an effect on me every time I glimpse it. I also love the views across the Tyne. I remember recently walking from Newcastle Quayside to George Stephenson's cottage at Wylam – the river views are wonderful up there.

My primary school days at Benton Park were everything you'd want them to be, most of the time. Charging

The Auf Wiedersehen, Pet *Geordies – Neville, Dennis and Oz – sail home from Germany in 1983*

around the playground blissfully unaware of the big, bad world that awaited me and my pals. The rude awakening came with secondary school, and Manor Park. I detested it from day one and it me. Some teachers took pleasure in dishing it out to the kids. It's now gone, with housing having taken the place of the classrooms, and good riddance.

I came through my formative years during the late Fifties and Sixties, the latter being arguably the most exciting decade in the history of the universe. As kids we'd gather on the grass outside our houses on a Saturday afternoon to discuss whichever latest records had just been played on TV's *Juke Box Jury*. Every week brought

Jimmy as Jed Shepperd in BBC TV's Crocodile Shoes *in 1994*

"Walking from Newcastle Quayside to George Stephenson's cottage at Wylam – the river views are wonderful up there."

"As a kid I would stand among the thousands of cloth-capped men crammed into the Leazes End, all of us cheering our beloved Magpies on."

at least one future classic. At 14 we'd go to local youth clubs to watch mates who were in groups (it was the Seventies before they took to calling themselves bands). I always wanted to get up and sing but hadn't a clue as to how you went about it. At 15 we'd walk tall and pile down to the Rex in Whitley Bay. It could be lively, especially if the local lads detected a townie. I remember seeing a band one Friday night called The Gobi Desert Canoe Club – how could you forget that name? – and their singer was Brian Johnson.

The first LP I remember buying – they were called long players back then – was *Road Runner* by Junior Walker & The All Stars, around 1968. Walker was a Tamla Motown sax player who'd had a break-out hit with *Road Runner.* Fantastic album. I can't remember where I bought it. It must've been somewhere in the town. First single was – I think – Jimi Hendrix's *All Along The Watchtower* in 1970. Bought it at the Charnwood shops in Longbenton.

My *Auf Wiedersehen, Pet* auditions have been well documented. I was the unlikely but extremely grateful recipient of one of the finest, funniest parts ever to be written for television, or anywhere else. It seems like a lifetime ago, and it was. October 2013 was the 30th anniversary of the first episode going out on ITV. If I watch a bit of it these days I see only a clumsy young man charging around like a bull in a china store. The guys really looked after me.

It felt odd coming back to Newcastle to play the City Hall with the *Crocodile Shoes* tour in 1995 to a venue I'd been in many times but never looking out from the stage. It was a great night, the first of many I've had there. I played Newcastle Arena not long after. I remember my mum told me off afterwards for swearing!

The North East people who make me laugh most are Rowan Atkinson, Ant & Dec, Brian Johnson – who could, in another life, have been a stand-out stand-up – Brendan Healy and Tony Blair (for all the wrong reasons). I'm also a great admirer (in no particular order) of George and Robert Stephenson, Mark Knopfler, Basil Bunting, Lord Armstrong, Jack Common, Alan Hull, Raymond Black, Chas Chandler, Ian La Frenais, Lord (Peter) Taylor, Pat Barker, Alan Shearer, Eric Burdon, Cheryl Cole, Lee Hall, Peter Flannery, Sting and Peter Beardsley.

"St James' Park, in all its guises past and present, has figured large throughout my life."

HER GRACE

the Duchess of Northumberland

The Duchess of Northumberland is the visionary behind The Alnwick Garden, one of the most exciting contemporary gardens developed in the last century. She has overseen a full restoration of Alnwick Castle – seen as Hogwarts in the Harry Potter films – and is also the Lord Lieutenant of Northumberland. Between them, the Duke and the Duchess are patron or president of over 150 charities in the region.

WE MOVED TO NORTHUMBERLAND in 1986 and I thought it was magical and a fantastic place to bring up a family. There was plenty to do and I could pick my four children up from school and give them a picnic tea on the beach, which I often did. I have two sons and two daughters and I am proud of them all. They are great people who I would be honoured to call my friends. They're each very different but they all have good values and are their own people.

When I first came to the North East I found that everyone was incredibly warm and friendly and, as I've come to understand the people from the region more, what I especially appreciate is how they call a spade a spade. They say it as it is and I value and respect such honesty and frankness.

Obviously The Alnwick Garden has been the major project of my lifetime and I know that it has brought pleasure to people of all ages, which makes me happy when I watch them. But it's not something I've ever felt proud of: I still haven't completed what I said I would do and maybe when I've finished it I'll appreciate that I've made a small difference.

Once a forgotten and derelict plot, the Garden has been transformed into an exciting and educational space, dancing with water and ringing with the sounds of life. The Garden is recognised not only for gardening excellence, but also as a transformational project using its resources to provide real, measurable benefit for the people within the local community and visitors from every corner of the world. I am particularly interested in natural poisons and aphrodisiacs and have built one of the only poison gardens in the world in which every plant is a killer.

Alnwick Castle is a wonderful place with or without Hogwarts but in these days when marketing is vital to any successful business the Harry Potter factor was a great bonus.

I do lead a busy life and, to wind down, I go for long walks with my Italian Spinone dog, Fuzzy. One of my favourite views in Northumberland is from a viewpoint at the top of Hulne Park on the outskirts of Alnwick where we've made a graveyard. It'll be a wonderful place to be buried.

www.alnwickcastle.com

www.alnwickgarden.com

"The Alnwick Garden has been the major project of my lifetime and I know that it has brought pleasure to people of all ages."

ALAN PRICE

musician

Alan Price was the original keyboard player of The Animals, and his distinctive arrangement and organ playing on House of the Rising Sun *helped the band to their first No. 1 in 1964. He later worked with keyboardist Georgie Fame and had a big solo hit with* Jarrow Song *in 1974.*

I GREW UP IN FATFIELD in County Durham and, after my father was killed in an industrial accident at BOC, we moved to my granny's in Jarrow. I went to the Ellison School and passed the 11-plus then went to Jarrow Grammar.

I had my first band there, a skiffle group called the Black Diamonds. There was a better piano player than me at the school called Frankie Hedley so I played bass.

We used to go over to Newcastle and there was a hip vicar who used to have a rock'n'roll evening called Byker Parish Rock Club.

I remember this bunch of guys walked in one night looking like Gene Vincent & His Blue Caps with striped corduroy caps and blue-and-black striped shirts. They were called The Pagans and it was Eric Burdon and Johnny Steel. I was asked to sit in with them and play piano because I never got a chance in Frankie Hedley's group. Burdon said: "Why don't you join The Pagans?" So I hung out with them a while. In those days there was a lot of cross-fertilisation. It was like professional footballers being transferred between different clubs.

I also played keyboards and sang with Chas Chandler's group The Kon-Tors – he had a penchant for strange spellings – and we played every hit in the Top 30.

We would play in Newcastle at the Downbeat, in Carliol Square, and Club A'Gogo, on Percy Street, starting at midnight and finishing at 5am.

I'm told that Bryan Ferry and a bunch of other kids used to come down with their sleeping bags. As we were packing up the gear they would be getting into their sleeping bags with their girlfriends for a bit of a grope.

Picture courtesy of John Steel

Alan on keyboards with The Animals

The groups grew up with their fans in those days. We made our first EP at the Club A'Gogo and sold about 600 around the North East.

We played the Odeon too which they later turned into a blooming bingo hall. We saw the Everly Brothers on tour with Bo Diddley, and The Stones were also on the bill. The whole tour bus ended up at the Club A' Gogo and we had a battle of the bands with The Stones. We had the home crowd advantage so we blew them away.

Characters like Mickie Most, who had Rak Records and Ronan O' Reilly, who started Radio Caroline, were sniffing around. It was like the gold rush. It was a very exciting time. We became The Animals in 1963 and went

"I have quite a few favourite North East places. The view from the pram was Penshaw Monument, of course."

down to London to play. We were The Alan Price Combo before but Ronan knew all about PR and said that name doesn't make anybody turn around.

At the time Eric Burdon and myself were court musicians to a bunch of rough and ready guys called The Squatters. They were forerunners of Hell's Angels.

They had been chucked out of all the youth hostels in the North East. The only way to get a cheap drink – and drink all day – in those days was to go to the market towns in Northumberland where the pubs were open for the farmers.

That's what we would do. I used to play piano and Eric used to sing for The Squatters and their leader was called Animal Hogg – a fearsome guy with a couple of Alsatians. Eric related this story to Ronan so we became The Animals.

Of course, we had absolutely nothing in common. We were completely different types. None of us were from the same area. Burdon and Chas Chandler were from Newcastle, John Steel was from Gateshead, Hilton Valentine was from North Shields. But the group was greater than the bunch of individuals in it. There was a lot of talent in there but it was like a stagecoach with a horse in each corner all pulling in different directions. We were a good group and as a band we were powerful. There was an aggressiveness about us. We didn't have The Stones' foppishness. We were working class and closer to whatever the blues was about.

I miss the North East, of course, but you make a new life for yourself. I left the area effectively in 1963 so I've lived down south since. I still play Newcastle City Hall these days but the city doesn't seem to have that quality I remember of old Grey Street and Northumberland Street. Now everything is pedestrianised it seems to have lost its vitality.

If I do ever get a bit of time up there I like to have a wander around Jarrow. But where I used to live in Russell Street is the start of the Tyne Tunnel now. I sometimes go to Fatfield where I was born – it's very pretty down by the River Wear there.

I have quite a few favourite North East places. The view from the pram was Penshaw Monument, of course! And I remember going on a caravan holiday with my cousin Barry up to Bamburgh and Seahouses.

South Shields has fond memories because when I was growing up you couldn't take a girl back home. You would take a tent down to the beach so I remember Marsden Rock well!

I also traced my family back to Prices who lived at Old Low Light – the old lighthouse in North Shields – in the early 1800s. So although I've been a Sunderland fan all my life I'm a Geordie with ancestors going back to the mouth of the Tyne.

The winning goal in Sunderland's famous 1973 FA Cup Final 1-0 victory over Leeds United

I'll never forget the day Sunderland won the FA Cup in 1973. I was there. I flew back from Los Angeles for it and even forecast the result when I had an argument with Jackie Charlton who was also invited there by the BBC.

I went to a hotel in Piccadilly after the game and there was a cabaret band on and I got up and played with them. Len Shackleton and Jackie Milburn were there dancing with their partners. They brought the cup over to me and it was full of champagne. I drank champagne out of the FA Cup.

I had my head in my hands because I was hung over. I had been drinking all the way over from Los Angeles. Then I went straight into the hospitality suite for the BBC at Wembley and drank there too. When Ian Porterfield scored I had my head in my hands for a different reason. I just stared at the floor and I prayed. My brother John was watching it on TV – he was also a Sunderland supporter. I phoned him up and said: "Did you watch it? It was good wasn't it?" He said: "I was watching it, but my behind was nipping the buttons off the sofa!"

CHRIS RAMSEY

actor and stand-up comedian

Chris left university early to focus on stand-up comedy in 2007 (to the delight of his parents!), but his career went from strength to strength, with national live solo tours, TV and radio show appearances and the starring role in the award-winning BBC series Hebburn *set near his hometown of South Shields.*

I MOVED TO MANCHESTER for a few years when my stand-up career was taking off and it was fine, but now I've moved back to the North East, not far from where I grew up. It's such a novelty for my mates and my mam and dad to be able to just pop over to see me. There's something so comforting about it.

When I lived away I would get nostalgic about the area. We have some brilliant sights and things to do. I'd see adverts about visiting Scotland and think that we have places that are just as beautiful up here. The coastline is fantastic – it's just a shame we don't have the weather to go with it. When I think back to when I was a kid the things I remember best are the days out my mam and dad would take me on. Often we'd get the ferry to North Shields and have fish and chips and play pitch and putt. I used to love St Mary's Lighthouse and Souter Lighthouse. We'd also go to the Hancock Museum and the Science Museum in Newcastle. The Centre for Life opened too late for me to go as a kid but I bet it's brilliant. They'd let me in to play with all the stuff now, right?

The beach at Shields has the best memories for me. I remember having great summers there when I was at school and later with my mates from college – then we did get the weather. Swimming and just hanging out. It's a shame you have to grow up and start work and not be able to live like that any more!

I think the region is really special in all sorts of ways, but what makes it for me is the people. There's a sense of community and a great sense of humour, possibly the best in the UK. No one knows how to laugh at themselves like us lot. I travel all over the place and the audiences back home are the best.

It's a real point of pride for me that I can fill the Theatre Royal in Newcastle. I can't get over the fact that so many people would want to come and listen to me – it's honestly mind-blowing. It's a great theatre. I used to go and watch pantos there as a kid with my mam at Christmas, and now it's me people queue up for – it's amazing.

Another dream come true for me was getting the lead part of Jack on *Hebburn*. The writer, Jason Cook, is a good mate of mine and he wrote a small part for me in the series – but then I got offered the big one. I was blown away. It was really fun filming on the streets of Hebburn where so many of my mates used to live. I was wearing a suit one day when we were filming a scene, and I had to walk down a street talking on my phone. Half way through the scene, one of my mates' dads was working across the road, fixing someone's windows. He didn't realise we were filming and when he saw me he shouted out, asking what I was doing wearing a suit! He'd obviously never seen me look that smart.

www.chrisramseycomedy.com

Souter Lighthouse, Whitburn

"We'd get the ferry to North Shields and have fish and chips and play pitch and putt."

ALAN REED

artist

At the age of four Alan Reed decided to become an artist, following in the footsteps of his father and grandfather. He is best known for his landscape watercolours – although he also paints in oils – and his works include views of the North East, especially Tyneside, Italy and Oman.

THE TYNE, TYNE VALLEY and Northumberland are where my roots are, where I belong. I was born in Dilston near Corbridge and have lived most of my life in Ponteland. I'm lucky enough in my work to do a lot of travelling, especially to the Middle East and Italy. I've seen some wonderful, picturesque places but, when I come back home and go to pick up my dog from kennels, I look around and realise it's just as beautiful here.

Every time I drive along the Military Road I'm amazed by the stunning views of the Tyne Valley and the iconic Hadrian's Wall. We also have some of the loveliest coastal scenes in Northumberland such as Dunstanburgh, Bamburgh and Lindisfarne. One of the spots I often visit is just past the Ship Inn at Newton-by-the-Sea. My wife Susan and I like to walk along the beach after enjoying a crab sandwich or kippers at the Ship Inn and look out at Dunstanburgh Castle. It's where I proposed to her.

I also love the urban landscape too, especially of Newcastle. Anyone who knows my work is well aware of the big part this city plays in my life. I've done many paintings of the bridges but I think my personal favourite is one of the Theatre Royal in the snow. There's a little girl with a red coat walking on Grey Street: that's my eldest granddaughter who provides a good focal point and a splash of colour in the otherwise quite monochromatic snow scene. I'm also fond of a watercolour I did of the Theatre Royal and Grey Street from the second floor of Waterstones, Emerson Chambers. It was featured on the television series *Show me the Monet* – a sort of *X Factor* for artists. I didn't win but I did sell the painting!

Painting has always played a big part in my life. My father is a professional artist, mostly of golf courses as golf is his passion, and my grandfather was also a gifted painter, although he didn't do it for a living. When I was four years old, I remember seeing my grandfather lying in bed, several days after he suffered a heart attack. He showed me a picture he had just painted of the great love in his life, Jesus Christ. A few days later my grandfather died. It wasn't the best painting in the world, but it was the one which has made the greatest impression on my life. It has always struck me that out of all the things in his life that were dear to him, he chose Jesus to paint.

 www.alanreed.com

"I like to walk along the beach and look out at Dunstanburgh Castle – it's where I proposed to my wife."

VIC REEVES

comedian, actor, presenter, painter and author

Vic's real name is Jim Moir, under which he sometimes appears. He has enjoyed enduring success with his Middlesbrough-born comedy partner Bob Mortimer, both on television – starting with Vic Reeves Big Night Out *– and on live tours. Vic also starred in the award-winning BBC TV comedy drama* Hebburn.

I HAVE HAPPY MEMORIES growing up in Darlington. I was always out all day playing and you would come in when it was dark. I never watched the telly. I was out over the fields and in the woods messing about with my mates.

I was born in Leeds but we moved to Darlington when I was five and lived in the Eastbourne area of the town. I went to Eastbourne Comprehensive. My dad worked as a linotype operator at The Northern Echo newspaper. I spent a lot of time as a kid mucking around near the railway line.

I remember thrashing some nettles with a stick one day – because that's what you do when you are a kid – and behind the nettles I found this inscribed stone block saying 'Darlington this way, Stockton this way'. It was from the old, now defunct, historic Darlington-Stockton Railway. My dad told his mate at work who dug it up and donated it to the Railway Museum.

I used to work on a local farm. My first job was cutting pigs' balls off. Then the farmer would serve them up for us at lunchtime, which I wasn't very happy about. I said I didn't really want them so he made me a bacon sandwich instead, but he never washed his hands so they were covered in pig s**t!

I did get well paid at the farm though. I was rich compared to my mates so I'd go down to the town on a Saturday afternoon and buy myself a record and a pair of loons – those pants were all the rage in the Seventies. I used to wear the two-tone split knee variety. I also had a green pair and a white pair.

When I was a kid, summer holidays would always be spent at places like Scarborough, Robin Hood's Bay – I love the view there – and Whitby. In fact I had a holiday recently there with my mam and my wife and kids. It was a real trip down memory lane. We had a great time and my kids enjoyed it too. My wife was bowled over by how friendly the people were too. We spent days at Robin Hood's Bay, Whitby, Dalby Forest near Pickering and Hutton-le-Hole. We even went to see the gannets at the RSBP reserve at Bempton Cliffs near Filey. I'm not a massive birdwatcher but if there are any birds around I'll have a look at them.

The first record I ever bought was *Space Oddity* by David Bowie but I got it by mistake. I thought I was getting *Space Odyssey* the film. I was really disappointed but my mates thought I was really cool when it went to number one in the charts. I didn't come clean, of course – I pretended I knew what was what.

When I was about 18 me and my mates clubbed together and bought a car between us for about £50. It was a Morris Traveller. There were five of us who all chipped in a tenner and bought this old bone-shaker although only one of us could drive. So we would take day trips to market towns like Reeth and Richmond and go to the pub and drink Theakston's beer.

The inspiration for my club singer routines came from those early days. I used to be in a band called Trout and we would play workingmen's clubs alongside these awful pub singers. We were a heavy rock band with long hair and I played the bass. We would play venues like Bowes Wine Cellar in Darlington. The place was so small you were in danger of knocking somebody's pint over if you tried to turn around with your guitar. There was another band on the bill called The Beautiful Losers that featured Chris Rea and we supported them.

I remember playing at this hard pub in Stockton one time and there was a mass brawl going on right in front of us. The manageress was trying to break up the fight with a pool cue. She said: "I don't like your music. Can you do any Elvis?" We said: "We don't do that type of music" and she flung us out.

We would go up to Newcastle City Hall to see our favourite bands like Be-Bop Deluxe and venues like The Mayfair where I saw Hawkwind. The Mayfair was great. Everybody used to drink tequila sunrises. They looked good but tasted awful.

My TV comic partner Bob Mortimer is from Middlesbrough but I actually met him in 1986 in Goldsmith's Tavern in New Cross in London where I was doing a new show called *Vic Reeves Big Night Out*. I was doing it for my mates and there were a lot of ex-pats from the North East who used to come along. This bloke from 'Boro called Kingy brought Bob along. I was doing a character called Tappy Lappy – I had these big planks on my feet and a Bryan Ferry joke mask on, doing a tap dance to pre-recorded sounds of pots and pans jangling.

I live in Kent now but I really miss the North Yorkshire moors – I love the bleakness and how dramatic the landscape is. My work is around London so it would be difficult to move back to the North East. But I'm always checking out the prices of holiday cottages. It would be nice to have a little bolt-hole up there.

"When I was a kid, summer holidays would always be spent at places like Scarborough, Robin Hood's Bay – I love the view there – and Whitby."

VISCOUNT RIDLEY

scientist, writer, businessman and member of the House of Lords

A world-renowned writer and businessman, Matt Ridley lives at Blagdon near Newcastle. He was founding chairman of the International Centre for Life in Newcastle and non-executive chairman of Northern Rock. His most spectacular project to date is the creation of Northumberlandia – a massive land sculpture in the form of a woman known as the Lady of the North.

IT'S A SPECIAL PLACE, the North East. I feel incredibly lucky to have been born here and to live here. It has its own character, partly because it's geographically isolated: there are pockets which are highly populated and then there is nothing for miles. It's an island surrounded by sheep!

It has a combination of beautiful countryside and a vibrant industrial past. You don't often get both together. I don't think this country would have been quite the industrial powerhouse it was without the North East. We provided the energy in the shape of coal and were at the very heart of developing and building engines. And now there's a lot of industrial regeneration going on, so we're re-inventing ourselves again.

When I think of my earliest childhood memory, it shows what I mean. We lived surrounded by countryside at Shotton Grange and I used to go to school in Jesmond. My mother would take me to school and we'd drive through Seaton Burn just as the night shift was ending at the pit and the day shift was starting. You'd see men coming out of the gates, their faces black with coal dust and then we'd drive through Wideopen where there were cables strung across the road for buckets of coal. I can recall all the paraphernalia of the pits, and I'm probably from one of the last generations to remember that.

Two other memories spring to mind from back then. One is of holidays in Seahouses. I can remember splashing around in rock pools and, for some reason, I can still see the wallpaper in the bedroom of the B&B where we used to stay. I also remember the winter of 1963 when I was five years old. It was one of the coldest, most extreme winters and it must have been really hard for adults to go about their business, but my main memory was of being dragged in a sledge behind my parents' Land Rover. Nobody seemed to worry much about safety in those days.

Fifty years later snow is still magical for me. When I first saw snow on Northumberlandia it was a great moment. She began life in September 2012 and now I've seen her in full sun, fog, snow and sleet, reflected in water, and, as time goes on, she will only get better as she becomes more and more part of the landscape. Other places have their chalk horses and other figures – we've got our Lady of the North. I really want her to be for the people of the area. If people decide to come and visit from New Zealand that's all well and good, but it's really for the community of Cramlington and nearby areas.

I didn't start out thinking: let's build a giant, eccentric 1.5 million-tonne woman – I had originally thought about a landscape map of the UK or Northumberland – but the designer Charles Jencks had other ideas and he convinced me. The curves, patterns and shapes mirror the landscape around and it just seemed right. Occasionally I'd wake up at night and wonder what we were doing but now I'm convinced we've done the right thing.

It's no surprise that Northumberlandia is my favourite view of the region. Because this is south-east Northumberland and quite flat, you can stand at the top, 40 metres high, and see the sea, Tyneside, Cross Fell, the Pennines, Simonside, the Cheviots, that wild sweep of land of the Border Reivers – marvellous. It's what Northumberland is all about – space.

www.northumberlandia.com

www.blagdonestate.co.uk

"Other places have their chalk horses and other figures – we've got our Lady of the North."

SIR BOBBY ROBSON 1933-2009

footballer, club manager and England manager

As a footballer, Sir Bobby played for Fulham, West Bromwich Albion, Vancouver Royals and England. His glittering career in football continued as manager at Fulham, Ipswich Town, PSV Eindhoven, Sporting Lisbon, Porto, Barcelona and finally Newcastle United. He was England manager from 1982-1990. He launched the Sir Bobby Robson Foundation cancer charity in 2008.

THEY SAY YOU CAN'T ESCAPE YOUR ROOTS and I've never wanted to. I've always been proud to be a North Easterner. This is where I'm from – where I belong. I was brought up in Langley Park, a former coal-mining village in County Durham. And ever since I was a boy I've supported Newcastle United. I've often said that I bleed black and white.

Yet I left the area when I was just a youngster to play for Fulham. Later my wife Elsie, also from Langley Park, joined me. We had a family and, after my playing career was over, I went into football management. There were many unforgettable years as a club manager, then being asked to be England manager was one of the proudest moments of my life. Some say it's a poisoned chalice but if you know what you're doing it can be a wonderful job, the pinnacle of a manager's career.

But with my job came travel and, later as manager of clubs in Europe, it obviously meant living overseas. That was no hardship, believe me. I liked living abroad, and I remember with particular fondness the time I was in charge at Barcelona. We lived nearby in Sitges, a lovely spot. I saw the sea every day and it was a great place in every way. We also really enjoyed our time in Portugal and Holland.

So, thanks to a long career, we'd been away from the North East for 50 years and, because of my job, we never thought we'd come back. Of course there was always the pull of friends and family, especially our three sons, in England. Sometimes Elsie would say: "When are we going to go back and smell the roses? When will we see the grandchildren?" I couldn't really give her an answer: in football you never know what's around the corner. Then the chance came up to manage Newcastle United and we did come back. Now we're home and it's the best thing we ever did. This is where we're from, where we belong and where we'll stay.

"Ever since I was a boy I've supported Newcastle United – I bleed black and white."

Elsie and I grew up in Langley Park. We met there, we courted there and the place still means so much to us. Although I was born in Sacriston, just a short distance away, we moved to Langley Park when I was very young and the village was my universe when I was little. I used to share a bedroom with my brothers and we would sleep top-to-toe. My father worked at the colliery and we never had much money but it was a happy life. He loved football and he would have been so proud to have seen me as manager of his beloved Newcastle United.

Looking back, football was always there waiting for me. I remember my early schooldays when I would get back home and play football in the back streets. It was safe for kids to play on roads then, as there were no cars around. When I say football, it could have been a tennis ball or a piece of coal or flint we would kick around – it didn't matter to us.

"My favourite view isn't a castle, or a spectacular coastline or an ancient, historic monument: it's the view of Langley Park."

Langley Park 1935 © Beamish Museum

"In those days when so many communities were based around collieries, the Big Meeting was huge."

There are some fantastic views in this region, but my favourite isn't a castle, or a spectacular coastline or an ancient, historic monument: it's the view of Langley Park. If you stand at the top of the hill just outside the village of Esh and look over the valley you can see everything that formed me. There are the 'Silly Steps' from the village up to the top of the hill. There are 109 steps, and I used to run up and down them as a way of training. You can see the house where I grew up, the house where Elsie grew up, my old school, the churchyard where my mother and father are buried. There's the place where the colliery used to be – where my dad and I worked. There was a pit-heap at one time which seemed like a mountain in those days. Then there's the building that was King's Picture House, the cricket pitch where I used to play and the football pitch that got me to Fulham. I love it.

One of my most abiding memories as a lad – aside from football – was the annual Durham Miners' Gala, which we called the Big Meeting, in July. It was one of the major events of the year and we would never miss it. It's amazing that, despite the fact that the coal-mining industry has more or less gone in the region, this great event still takes place without fail, with thousands of people taking part and lining the streets to watch the colliery bands. It's something that stirs your soul. In those days when so many communities were based around collieries, the Big Meeting was huge – something everyone would get involved in. In Langley Park we started off walking through the village with everyone out on the streets and cheering us on before we went on into Durham.

A great honour for me was when I played *The Last Post* at the cenotaph in Langley Park on Remembrance Sunday as the wreaths were laid. It was an emotional time for everybody, and a nerve-wracking task to be asked to perform, but I played my little heart out.

Returning to the North East to live after all these years, there's something comforting to see how the region has picked itself up and made a go of things in so many different areas that we never thought about when I was a boy and mining communities were everywhere, but it's sad that you cannot tell that there were once working pits in many places. All of the buildings and machinery are gone and there are expanses of grass covering the areas where so many people made their living underground. But other industries have sprung up and now Newcastle has become a glamorous leisure destination, with some wonderful cultural spaces like the Sage Gateshead – one of my favourites – just over the river. But it's the people that make this region. When we have friends to stay they always say how straight, honest, friendly and warm the people are.

There's a lot to be proud of in the North East and there are some iconic views that are known around the world. Just think of the fantastic bridges spanning the Tyne. I have had the honour of setting off the New Year's Eve fireworks and starting the Great North Run from those bridges. The Tyne Bridge is one of the things that most people who have moved away from the area probably think about and miss the most.

As a Durham boy another sight that's close to my heart is Durham Cathedral and Castle. When you arrive by rail, no matter how many times you've seen it, that view from the train window is almost enough to take your breath away.

And now we have a relatively new iconic view – the Angel of the North. What a sculpture. I love the fact that it stands on an area where previously generations of coal-miners toiled underground. I see it every day, and every day it reminds me that I'm home.

www.**sirbobbyrobsonfoundation**.org.uk

"The Tyne Bridge is one of the things that most people who have moved away from the area probably think about and miss the most."

"Every day I see the Angel of the North,
and every day it reminds me that I'm home."

BRYAN ROBSON OBE

footballer and football manager

Bryan Robson began his football career with West Bromwich Albion in 1972 before moving to Manchester United in 1981 where he became the longest-serving skipper in the club's history. He also managed Middlesbrough FC. He now works as an ambassador for Manchester United and lives in Cheshire with wife Denise.

MY EARLIEST MEMORIES are of when we lived in Witton Gilbert, a little pit village next to Langley Park where Sir Bobby Robson grew up. He always spoke so passionately about where he was from so it was a great honour for me to be his captain for England and help the team reach the 1990 World Cup finals. One of my first football matches as a kid was at Langley Park.

Courtesy of Bryan Robson

Left to right: Bryan, his father and sister Susan

My dad Brian called me Robbo. He worked as a long-distance lorry driver so he couldn't be there all the time, but whenever he could, he was there. In the early days if he was home at the weekend he would always take me and my sister Susan along with the family dog up to the local football pitch at the top of the hill in Witton Gilbert.

Then when I was six we moved to South Pelaw, in Chester-le-Street, and I still love that terrific view from the top of the hill looking over the town towards Lambton Castle with the River Wear down in the dip then back up the valley to the other side.

Lumley Castle makes a fantastic backdrop these days for Durham's first-class cricket matches at the Riverside, of course. Another very special view for me is Durham Cathedral and Castle. It's spectacular and gets me every time.

I was always captain of the school football teams, first for Chester-le-Street Primary School then Birtley Comprehensive and also the Washington and District team.

In those days my mam Maureen used to take me and my team-mates to all of the games in her Austin Westminster. That's continued even to this day as she still takes my brothers' boys to their school football games. She's a fanatical football fan.

Football was all I ever wanted to do and it has given me an incredible life. I also owe a big debt to my PE teacher Bill Chapman. I was told I was too small to make it as a professional footballer and he used to stay behind at school and do extra work on my fitness, giving me a weights routine to build up my strength.

My mam and dad were both Newcastle United fans and that became my team too, but the first professional match I ever went to was to see Man Utd play Sunderland in the FA Cup. It was the great Man Utd team that had Bobby Charlton, Dennis Law and George Best and they won. My first Newcastle game was against Northampton Town in the old second division. I've still got the programme to this day.

The buzz at St James' Park was incredible and I was hooked. I would go with my dad like Bobby Robson went to matches with his dad. If we got there early he would park me on the wall at the front of the wing paddock and go for a couple of pints. It was all standing apart from a few posh seats in those days. If you got there late the blokes used to pass the youngsters on their shoulders down to the front so you would get a good view.

This was the Sixties and I was a big fan of the captain Bobby Moncur and centre forward Wyn Davies. When it came to choosing a football club I plumped for West Brom and joined as an apprentice at 15 on £5 a week. There was interest from Newcastle and Burnley too and I had trials for both but it just didn't feel right at Newcastle for whatever reason. I just didn't enjoy it there. West Brom really looked after the youngsters. They made you feel really welcome and you trained with the first team unlike a lot of other teams at the time.

It's a bit unfortunate that I never played for Newcastle. Actually when I was older and coming to the end of my career with Man Utd it crossed my mind, but I was 38 by then and Newcastle had a great team under Kevin Keegan. They were challenging Man Utd for the title and I was a little bit too old. If they had been struggling at the bottom of the table I might have got a couple of years with them.

I still get back to the North East a few times a year. Sadly my dad died of cancer in 2003 but my mam still lives in the same house where I grew up and I always stay

"Lumley Castle makes a fantastic backdrop these days for Durham's first-class cricket matches at the Riverside."

Bryan Robson with England manager Bobby Robson at the 1986 Mexico World Cup

Bryan was Manchester United's longest-serving captain

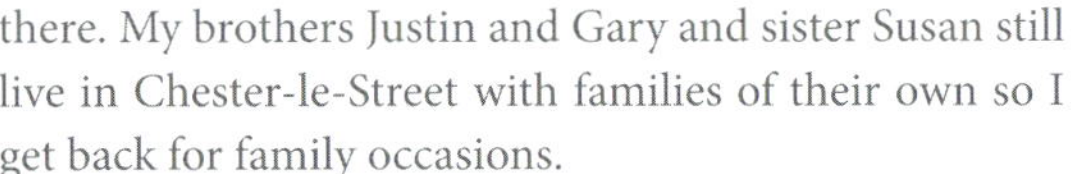

there. My brothers Justin and Gary and sister Susan still live in Chester-le-Street with families of their own so I get back for family occasions.

Sir Bobby was a great England manager to play for. He was unbelievably passionate – like his friend Sir Alex Ferguson – about the game. He lived and breathed football and could talk about it all day long. I don't think people gave him enough credit as England manager. Tactically he was brilliant and a great man-manager. He was always asking me if the players were happy. He showed genuine concern for everyone. He was also brave enough to go abroad and take on another challenge and all his experience in Europe made him a better England manager.

Loads of people used to think he was my dad, though, because we had the same surname. The England lads used to have a running joke about Bobby the manager and his son the captain. They used to take the mickey and say: "Ah, Dad's picked you again."

It was great to see him come back to his home club and manage Newcastle for his final job. That job was always in his heart. He was a Newcastle supporter like myself and he famously said he bled black and white.

"I still love that terrific view from the top of the hill looking over the town towards Lambton Castle with the River Wear down in the dip then back up the valley to the other side."

FRANC RODDAM

film director, screenwriter, TV producer and publisher

Hollywood director Franc Roddam, from Norton-on-Tees, made his name with the iconic 1979 movie Quadrophenia *and based the ITV comedy drama* Auf Wiedersehen, Pet *on his life-long friend Mick Connell. He lives in Notting Hill, London with wife Leila, daughters Sidonie and Zazou, and son Zane.*

I GREW UP AT 71 DARLINGTON LANE, and out of our living-room window we could see across the fields to Stockton and in the background the Cleveland hills and Roseberry Topping. It played a big part in our lives. It started for me as a child, just looking out the window. I was one of seven children. John, the eldest, has passed away now, sadly. Then there was Bernard, Vincent, Peter, David, me, then my sister Angela – the youngest. David and I would climb it from the age of 11.

We thought it was a mountain. It did have a beautiful shape – it was nicknamed the Matterhorn of Middlesbrough – but it was a molehill really. The countryside is stunning around Great Ayton and from the top you can see all the way to Captain Cook's Monument.

"That's Mick and me posing in the high street in Stockton. We thought we were being very funny. It's the Sixties and we look like the Likely Lads."

As a teenager, when I was working as an apprentice in the shipyards we used to free-climb up one of its rock faces. It was quite sheer and about 80 feet high. Even 30 feet off the ground was terrifying.

When I got older and moved away I would always come back home for Christmas. We would have loads to eat and get hammered and on Boxing Day it was a hangover cure to walk to the top in the snow.

My best pal Mick Connell – he was the inspiration for *Auf Wiedersehen, Pet* because he went out and worked as a brickie in Germany – and one or two of my brothers would climb it. By the time we had done that we were ready to start eating and drinking all over again.

More recently I have taken my wife Leila and two daughters Sidonie and Zazou to see the area and Roseberry Topping. So it is still a part of my life even though I live in London. I miss the landscape and, most of all, the people. My brother Bernard still lives at the foot of Roseberry Topping and my other brothers Vincent and Peter are still in the North East.

I remember back in the early Sixties Mick and I used to go to Stockton Folk Club on a Monday night and there was this local bard Graeme Miles who wrote great songs. Lots of them have stayed with me and I still sing lines from them to my children like:

"The rolling Cleveland Hills
The green-brackened Clevelands
The red-iron Clevelands are the dearest of all."

He also wrote a terrific song about getting back from Guisborough late at night after a night on the tiles. It was called *Along the Guisborough Road* and the lyrics went:

"Four miles to travel along the Guisborough Road.
Past the Cross Keys ensign, now the sleet has turned to snow
Four miles to travel along the Guisborough Road."

Mick and I identified with it because we did it many times. If you had been to a dance chasing girls and missed the last bus the only way was to walk home. It was an exposed road and it always seemed to be in the howling wind and the snow. We would be dressed in the sharpest Italian suits but never an overcoat – no good if you got in a fight. And we'd invariably walk barefoot because we didn't want to ruin our highly polished patent-leather shoes.

Another Teesside landmark that always intrigued me was the Transporter Bridge. It has a natural beauty about it, framed against the skyline. And the scale of it was awe-inspiring as a child. I love the Angel of the North for the same reason. It has a powerful quality.

I had the idea of taking *Auf Wiedershen, Pet* to America for the third series and came up with the plot to dismantle the Transporter and re-assemble it in Arizona. So we had these cowboy builders in the desert selling a bridge to the Red Indians and uniting the tribes of the disenfranchised Geordie working class and the Native Americans. I had done computer-generated imagery for the film *Moby Dick* so I knew we could dismantle it by trickery. The problem was some people thought it was for real when they saw it on TV and started a 'save our bridge' campaign.

"Another Teesside landmark that always intrigued me was the Transporter Bridge. It has a natural beauty about it, framed against the skyline. And the scale of it was awe-inspiring as a child."

PAUL RODGERS

singer and musician

Paul Rodgers is one of the finest rock singers of his generation. He will always be remembered for the single All Right Now, *which took the charts by storm in 1970, became a worldwide hit and propelled his band Free to pop stardom. He later enjoyed success with Bad Company and as a solo artist as well as touring and recording with Queen.*

MIDDLESBROUGH WAS A VERY GRITTY, grimy place when I was a kid because of all the heavy industry, and, of course, most of that has gone now. I remember saying to my kids: "You'll be really surprised when you visit Middlesbrough because you live in a really nice place." But of course it's like a park now – all green and the air is clean – so they wondered what I was on about!

I grew up in Valley Road in Grove Hill, Middlesbrough. We lived at number 25, two doors down from the legendary football manager Brian Clough. I went to school at St Joseph's and then St Thomas's.

I used to go to Ayresome Park and watch 'Boro when I was a kid. I was really shocked when I found out they had knocked it down. I used to go to the match with my mate Pete Smith. He's my best friend and we are still in touch. We have known each other from even before you have childhood memories because our mothers used to park us side by side in our prams with them chatting away. That's how far we go back!

Pete became a fireman. He's still up in the North East. As kids we always used to knock around together. We would go down to the park and play football, muck about and make a nuisance of ourselves. We would go over to the fire station and climb up on the windows and look at the fire engines and dream of being firemen and he actually did become one.

I was just 17 when I left and I've travelled the world since. But my roots are still there and I still have lots of friends and relatives there. They always come to the North East shows and it's great to catch up with everyone. I'm stamped through with the North East just like you are when you come off the northern assembly line

Courtesy of Paul Rodgers

Free in 1968 – left to right Simon Kirke, Andy Fraser, Paul Kossoff and Paul Rodgers

– and it's never going to go away.

I started playing music as a kid at school with our band The Roadrunners. Colin Bradley was the guitarist in the band and his older brother Joe took us under his wing and managed us when we were only about 13 or 14. Even then we were quite a well-organised little unit. We had our own van and our equipment was all paid for. So as soon as we finished school we were off doing shows all over the place. We did workingmen's clubs, weddings, gigs anywhere we could get them. I was playing bass in those days as well as singing. I was pretty much self-taught. My grandfather worked on the railways and used to play the banjo but I don't remember anyone else in the family being very musical.

I listened to a lot of blues in my childhood. It was a very strong influence on me. I would listen to John Lee

"When I was a kid Pete Smith's parents would take us up to where Cook's Monument is and we used to look down at Middlesbrough from up there and all the rows and rows of houses. I remember saying to his mum: "It looks small, doesn't it?" And she said: "Maybe it is." And that changed my view on life. It was one of the triggers that put it into my mind to go and make my way in music."

Hooker, Sonny Boy Williamson, Muddy Waters, Howlin' Wolf. These guys were heavy-duty blues performers and they sang about this earthy other world where chickens ran in the streets, kids played barefoot and people jumped on railroad trains with their guitars and travelled thousands of miles to play their music. It was a completely different world to the world I came from and knew, and when I looked around my hometown I was drawn to this romantic world.

When I was a kid Pete Smith's parents would take us up to where Cook's Monument is and we used to look down at Middlesbrough from up there and all the rows and rows of houses. I remember saying to his mum: "It looks small, doesn't it?" And she said: "Maybe it is." And that changed my view on life. It was one of the triggers that put it into my mind to go and make my way in music.

My favourite singer has to be Otis Redding. He has been a huge influence on me. He sang from the heart. He had gospel roots and he really had soul. I remember being 13 or 14 and you go through a lot of angst and uncertainty at that age as you are becoming a man with those huge hormone changes. Otis Redding was someone who really spoke to me. When he sang songs like *A Change is Gonna Come* and *Down in the Valley* it was so pure and so sincere. That's what I wanted to do.

I love the Newcastle City Hall. It's always had a great atmosphere and I have great memories of playing there in the early days with Free. There's so much history there on that stage. I also played there with Bad Company. Newcastle is such a great place to play but it's the fans that really create the brilliant atmosphere.

www.paulrodgers.com

Paul got Bad Company back together in 2009 and toured with them for the first time in 30 years

Music Now **on 11/7/1970 reported: 'Free were faced with riots when they played Durham Tech last weekend. Two thousand people barred their way to the stage, and when they eventually went on one-and-a-half-hours late, they were forced off again after one number. Police had to escort the group back to the hotel, where the riots continued. The group, whose single *All Right Now* is currently at Number 1 in the Music Now charts, fly to Germany and Holland on Thursday.'**

"I'm stamped through with the North East just like you are when you come off the assembly line – and it's never going to go away."

PAM ROYLE

broadcaster

Pam Royle is best known as a journalist and presenter of ITV News for Tyne Tees and the Border region. Pam has worked on many television programmes both regionally and nationally. She is also a voice coach and voice-over artist. She is a keen supporter of several charities and is a Deputy Lieutenant of County Durham.

OUT OF AFRICA AND INTO THE NORTH EAST – in a nutshell, that's the story of my early childhood. My father's job as an engineer had taken my family to South Africa for three years when I was a few months old, so my earliest memories are of playing in the sun, being surrounded by nature and my father's Hillman Sunbeam being chased by a buffalo on a trip to Kruger National Park.

When I was four we moved to Guisborough and I carried on living outdoors most of the time, like most children did then. I remember we used to go to Roseberry Topping a lot, climbing up from different sides, and collecting bilberries to make into jam. There was a lake at the bottom that our Dalmatian dog used to swim in. Really lovely, innocent days with no mod cons.

I love the Cleveland hills. I used to have a pony and would go out for hours on end round the hills with friends. I'd leave in the morning and stay out most of the day. My mother didn't know where I was, but no one worried about that in those days. If I wasn't with the pony I'd be cycling to villages like Hutton Rudby and Chopgate to see my friends.

The coast has played a big part in my childhood, especially in the south of the region where I still live. We used to go to Sandsend near Runswick Bay for weekends. We would pitch a tent on the beach, put up a windbreak and eat tinned salmon sandwiches. It was idyllic.

I still love the sea and spend as much time sailing – or just being near the sea – as possible. I'm a member of the Tees and Hartlepool Yacht Club which I really enjoy. It's not snooty at all – there are people there from all walks of life – and Hartlepool Marina has become one of my favourite places in the North East. As a family we have a jet-ski and I recently took part in a charity event for cerebral palsy, jet-skiing from Hartlepool to Whitby. It all ended a bit humiliatingly when we broke down and limped into Staithes where a great man – the harbourmaster, Captain Norman Fowler – helped us out. He has become a firm friend.

I love my job and it's wonderful to get feedback from viewers who appreciate what we do and say thank you for bringing us the news. It's a vast area to cover and, as anyone who works in television knows, it's a huge team effort. What you see on screen is just a part of it. Each show is a huge achievement every night.

While my work means so much to me, I get most satisfaction from working with charities. The two closest to my heart are the Great North Air Ambulance – which doesn't get any Government funding – and the Evening Chronicle's Sunshine Fund which I work on with Ant & Dec and the Paralympian Stephen Miller. It helps disadvantaged or disabled children and I have met some wonderful youngsters through the charity whose enthusiasm and determination is truly inspirational.

I'm particularly proud to be Deputy Lieutenant of County Durham, which means I sometimes deputise for the Lord Lieutenant, the Queen's representative. Every year I lay a wreath at the Remembrance Service at Sedgefield. During the time Tony Blair was Prime Minister, the protocol was that I would be ahead of him because, in that role, I trumped the PM!

It's a real privilege to be able to represent the North East in whatever capacity, though. I have worked and lived elsewhere but, for me, there is nowhere else like it. People here can laugh at themselves: they have a great sense of humour and there is tremendous resilience about them, no matter what is thrown at them. I'd like to see more people being recommended for honours for the work they do. I love the sense of community and identity we still have. It probably harks back to our industrial heritage but it's still there, intact. I hope we keep it.

Roseberry Topping in the spring

www.gov.uk/honours

www.sunshine-fund.org

www.greatnorthairambulance.co.uk

"I'm a member of the Tees and Hartlepool Yacht Club, and Hartlepool Marina has become one of my favourite places in the North East."

ALAN SHEARER OBE

footballer

Alan was a star striker for Southampton, Blackburn Rovers – where he won the Premier League title – and Newcastle United. He captained the English national team as well as Newcastle. The record goalscorer for the Premier League and Newcastle United, he retired as a player in 2006 and became a BBC football pundit. He founded the Alan Shearer Foundation in 2012 and is a patron of the Sir Bobby Robson Foundation.

I WAS BORN IN GOSFORTH and 99 per cent of my childhood was spent there. I lived in a street called Park Avenue in a three-bedroom council house. I was extremely happy there. I played football every day outside on the road or in the local park. I could walk to all three of my schools (Grange, Gosforth Central and Gosforth High) and I played for all my school teams at those schools.

Most of my best memories are around football, as you can imagine. I vividly remember watching Newcastle at a young age. I was there for Kevin Keegan's debut and I was a ball boy for his last game at St James' Park. It was then that I decided that one day I wanted to play in front of that crowd.

As a family we went up the coast every summer to Amble and stayed in a caravan. I remember walking up the beach in a woolly hat and duffle coat in the middle of July because it was so cold! I'm sure we spent most of our time riding bikes, playing football and losing our money in the arcades.

The North East is very special because of the people. They are the ones that make it special. They are hard-working, honest and open. I moved away in 1986 to Southampton and came back in 1996 and I'd be surprised if I were ever to move away again. It was my dream to play for Newcastle. I love living here, it's a lovely area, the nightlife is great, there is loads to do, great golf courses – and my son was born here.

I have one favourite place – it's called St James' Park – so many great memories there.

© NUFC

"I have one favourite place – it's called St James' Park – so many great memories there."

Dawn breaks on the Close House driftwood horse

Ant & Dec with Alan and two youngsters from the centre

Close House is 'my' golf club. It's a new course, only three years old, and has a great clubhouse and atmosphere and I spend a lot of time there. I also love all the links courses up the coast.

Another favourite place for me is the Alan Shearer Centre – St Cuthberts Care's specialist provision for people with complex disabilities. I donated my testimonial money to enable people with disabilities and their families to have access to the best sensory facilities and activities possible. In 2012 I set up the Alan Shearer Foundation to help raise funds for the centre, and I like to spend as much time there as I can. It's also something the area should be very proud of, as it is the only one of its kind in our region.

www.alanshearercentre.org.uk

"Close House is 'my' golf club. It's a new course, only three years old, has a great clubhouse and atmosphere and I spend a lot of time there."

JEFF STELLING

broadcaster

Jeff Stelling started his career as a journalist on the Hartlepool Mail before moving into broadcasting. He presents Gillette Soccer Saturday *for Sky Sports and is well known as a long-suffering supporter of his beloved Hartlepool United FC. Jeff, who has been named Sports Broadcaster of the Year for five successive years, lives in Hampshire with his family.*

I WENT TO RIFT HOUSE JUNIOR SCHOOL and West Hartlepool Grammar School for Boys. My home was in Catcote Road, which these days is one of the main thoroughfares in the town, but in those days came to a dead end 50 yards past my house. It gave way to glorious countryside and farmland and we would spend many weekend and holiday days walking through the countryside to Dalton Piercy and Elwick. At the right time of the year it was also ideal for brambling. An early morning start was essential to get the pick of the best – only the best would do for my mam's bramble and apple pie!

Most of the rest of the time would be spent playing football and cricket on the playing fields at nearby Chaucer Avenue. I won more Test matches there than Nick Cook can ever dream of and scored more winning goals at Wembley finals than even Roy of the Rovers. It was a lovely community, everyone knew each other, no one locked their doors, no fear of being allowed to play outside in the dark even at a young age.

My mum is in her 90s now and still lives in the same house in Catcote Road. One of my brothers lives not too far away and I have nieces, nephews, aunts and uncles dotted around the region. These days, with a family of my own and work commitments it's hard to get back as often as I would like, but I do try and make it home half a dozen times or so each year.

My sons Rob and Matt had visited the town before but their first real memory of it was around 2006 when they were seven and eight. We stayed at the Staincliffe Hotel overlooking the North Sea and even though the weather was pretty awful, they loved it. We played football on the beach in the rain, went to the Historic Quay

Jeff with his Soccer Saturday *Sky pundits*

and enjoyed the town's hospitality and good restaurants – there weren't any when I was a boy or even a young man. I remember Rob asking: "Why can't we live here dad?" which went down well with me – but not with his mum Liz, who is a Wimbledon girl!

They both love football and Rob always wears his Hartlepool shirt to training with Winchester. We went to Stevenage to see them in April 2013 and I can vouch he is as fanatical as me. My first game was in the early Sixties at the Vic, when I went with my sister Sue. I remember we won – which didn't happen often – and we walked home, braving an icy cold wind and made toast around the coal fire while watching black-and-white TV. The only snag would be the toast would often fall off the fork into the fire and your toasting hand would be burning, but it was a family ritual.

"There's a fantastic view I love from Seaton Carew looking across Seal Sands. You have the natural beauty of the sea and expanses of golden sand but the industrial landscape in the background reminds you it is a place where a lot of people have put in a lot of hard graft."

The famous Hartlepool monkey sculpture at the Quay

Jeff is a life-long Hartlepoool United fan, and takes every opportunity to show his team colours on television

Obviously over the years there have been many more downs than ups as a Pools fan. I know a lot of people would say the League One play-off final against Sheffield Wednesday in 2005 would be among the best games they've seen, but for me it was the worst – we lost! The best may well have been the second leg of the semi-final that same year at Tranmere. I still remember hiding behind the sofa as Ritchie Humphreys scored the winner in the penalty shoot-out and screaming so loudly that my wife galloped down from the bedroom, thinking I had been attacked.

My Middlesbrough rant – when I defended the town on *Gillette Soccer Saturday* after it was pilloried in a 2007 TV poll as the worst place to live in Britain – still gets played at most of the events I go to. I am staggered with the effect it has had. Every town has good and less good areas, but people stereotype the north shockingly. I remember I was set to film a piece in Hartlepool before that 2005 play-off final and the young producer I was with wanted to see boarded-up terraced houses, rag-and-bone men with their horses and carts and so on. I took him to the beach, to St Hilda's on the headland and to Camerons Brewery. He left with a much better idea of what the town is like. The 'Boro rant was another chance to try and change people's perceptions.

I still feel the North East is home – I miss the football club, the beaches but most of all the people. When I do come home total strangers, taxi drivers and barmen treat me like their best friend – I love the fact that though I live a long way away I am still one of them and always will be.

I have so many favourite North East places: The Vic, of course, the beach at Seaton and Longscar Rocks which evoke memories of a lot of chilly family picnics in August and icy swims in the North Sea, Seaton Carew Golf Club, the North Yorkshire Moors, Robin Hood's Bay and Redcar Racecourse! Who needs 80 degrees in Palma when you could have 50 degrees in Pontefract?

There's a fantastic view I love from Seaton Carew looking across Seal Sands. You have the natural beauty of the sea and expanses of golden sand but the industrial landscape in the background reminds you it is a place where a lot of people have put in a lot of hard graft.

I remember finding the transition to working in London tough at first – one listener to LBC Radio complained my accent was a speech defect – but ironically now people often say they recognise me first by my voice and accent. Nowadays TV is littered with regional accents, so in some ways I was almost an accidental pioneer. But it's absolutely right that people broadcasting to the whole nation should speak in accents representative of the whole nation – whether it's Scouse, Scottish, Brummie, Welsh, Geordie or Hartlepudlian!

"I still feel the North East is home – I miss the football club, the beaches but most of all the people. When I do come home total strangers, taxi drivers and barmen treat me like their best friends – I love the fact that though I live a long way away I am still one of them and always will be."

STING CBE

musician, songwriter and actor

Sting is a composer, singer, bassist, actor and activist. A prolific songwriter, he has collected ten Grammy Awards and two Brits for his solo work. With The Police Sting earned five Grammys and two Brits and in 2003 the band was inducted into the Rock and Roll Hall of Fame. Sting has also received a Golden Globe, an Emmy, three Oscar nominations and in 2004 he was named the MusiCares Person of the Year.

I WAS BORN AND RAISED IN WALLSEND – something I am very proud of. We lived on Gerald Street, which is gone now, and at the end of our street was the Swan Hunter shipyard. The ships they built there were some of the largest ships ever constructed. My first memories as a child growing up in those streets are of this surreal industrial landscape. That image of the ship at the end of our street is emblazoned in my mind. The men would walk past our door every day on their way to work on these mighty ships, and they'd enter the shipyard – a terrifying and noisy theatre of iron and steel. And I used to wonder if that would be my destiny too.

Some of the most vivid memories of my childhood are of the launchings of the ships built in Wallsend. It was a major thing in the community. We'd all go. I remember standing on the pavement waving my Union Jack as the Queen Mother drove past in her Rolls-Royce. There would be speeches and a bottle thrown at the ship. It seemed like the most glamorous thing in the world to me as a child.

I saw my first movies at The Ritz – Fess Parker in *Davy Crockett*, and Doris Day in *Please Don't Eat The Daisies*. On Saturday mornings they screened children's cartoon serials, which was a great treat for us.

My mother brought rock and roll into the house on records of black acetate with brightly coloured labels from MGM, RCA, Decca – Little Richard, Jerry Lee Lewis and Elvis. I was mesmerised. I first heard The Beatles in my final year at St Columba's Primary School – the first bars of *Love Me Do* had an immediate effect on all of us boys. I think we recognised something significant, even revolutionary in the sound. Lennon and

Sting, centre, back at Newcastle Central Station with The Police in 1983 following their world tour

The Esso Northumbria, *built in the Swan Hunter shipyard, was the largest ship in the world upon its launch in 1969*

McCartney were both grammar school boys from humble roots in the North who went on to conquer the world, and gave permission to a whole generation of others like me to attempt the same thing. Dylan was another big influence. I would listen to his records for hours memorising all of the lyrics. I also immersed myself in jazz. An older boy in school lent me two albums by Thelonious Monk. I would put one on while I did my homework and let it seep in. With Miles Davis and John Coltrane, I realised these were musicians exploring the outer reaches of human understanding. They had an enormous impact on me.

Braidford's, the music shop, was under the Gaumont Cinema in Wallsend and I was always in there mooching around, rummaging through record racks, and if I had enough money, buying guitar strings or sheet music. That's how I would spend most of my Saturdays. It was a magical place for me as a child.

There were so many great music clubs in Newcastle in those days. Music was everywhere – places like the Club A'Gogo, The Mayfair, and The Rex Hotel in Whitley Bay. I remember the excitement in town when Jimi Hendrix was booked to appear at the 'Gogo. He played two sets and I somehow managed to get in even though I was technically too young. There was a feeling amongst the crowd that we were about to witness an event of high

"There is a magnificent view in Tynemouth from the headland below the 11th-century abbey on the clifftop, looking down at the twin piers and lighthouses which sit like sentinels on either side of our famous river."

"So many talented musicians hail from the North East. I've been working with Kathryn Tickell for many years."

cultural significance. The night remains a blur of noise and breathtaking virtuosity. Afterwards, I lay in my bed wide awake with my ears ringing and my world view significantly altered.

Numerous bands thrived in the pubs and clubs of Newcastle, outfits that had played together since the Fifties – the River City Jazzmen, the Vieux Carré Jazzmen and the Phoenix Jazzmen. I played in all of these combos at one time or another and developed a deep fondness for their raucous harmony – every bit as exciting as rock and roll. On a Saturday night I would wear the pink nylon shirt of the Phoenix Jazzmen with pride as we played various workingmen's clubs – we played to miners in Cramlington, shipyard workers in Sunderland and chemical workers in Teesside.

The Newcastle Big Band was started in the late Sixties and was something of a local institution by the time I joined their ranks as a bass player. We played the upstairs room of the Gosforth Hotel, sharing the proceeds of the door money. Last Exit made our first recordings at Impulse Studios in Wallsend, coincidentally above Mr Braidford's music shop in the old Gaumont cinema. Mr Braidford was long dead by that time and his shop was boarded up, which was terribly sad.

My last gig in Newcastle before moving to London was with Last Exit at the Gosforth Hotel. The mood in the room seemed to be willing us on to greater things. The next day, a local TV station offered us a spot on the evening news to say goodbye to the area. We played my suitably ironic song, *Don't Give Up Your Daytime Job*. This was our first TV performance and I was so nervous I forgot the second verse, so I sang the first one twice. The North East will always feel like home, and I always enjoy coming back to visit. It is a unique place with a great creative atmosphere and legacy. Music is alive and it's part of people's lives. There are so many talented musicians who hail from the North East. I've been working with Kathryn Tickell for many years, of course. She is an extraordinary musician. And her brother Peter has recently joined my band and has been on the road with me. I've also been working with my old friend Jimmy Nail on my new record *The Last Ship*, which will also be staged as a play of the same name in 2014, as well as Brian Johnson and The Wilson Family from Teesside. And The Unthanks, who have such beautiful voices.

Sting on stage with The Police in 2007

www.sting.com

"My last gig in Newcastle before moving to London was with Last Exit at the Gosforth Hotel. The mood in the room seemed to be willing us on to greater things."

PAUL THOMPSON

drummer

Best known as drummer for Roxy Music from 1971-1980 and then from 2001, Paul has also played with John Miles (a fellow Jarrow lad), Gary Moore, Angelic Upstarts and US-based Concrete Blonde. Fans call him 'the great Paul Thompson' in tribute to his drumming skills and influence on other drummers.

LOOKING AT OLD PHOTOS OF JARROW where I grew up it's almost like something from Charles Dickens with the outside toilets, shared washing facilities and poss tubs. I remember all of that from when I was little. Now a lot of the area, including the street where we used to live until I was four, has gone – flattened to make way for the Tyne Tunnel.

A lot of my earliest memories are of sitting around the radio with my parents listening to music like skiffle, The Beatles and The Searchers. This was before we had television. It was great when I got my own transistor and I would listen to Radio Luxembourg late into the night.

I always liked the idea of drumming, although I had to make do with a Meccano set, cardboard boxes and biscuit tins before I convinced my parents to get me the real thing – although it was just one drum and a cymbal. We practised in a garden shed – that was when I was 11. At the age of 14 a few pals and I started a group called The Tyme, and we would practise and play in local youth clubs, getting our gear there in a wheelbarrow.

My parents wanted me to get a 'proper' job, so I started working in the shipyards when I left school at 15 but I never stopped playing. When I was 16 I auditioned for John Miles' band called The Urge. I got the job and it was a big leap for me after playing youth clubs. So I was working during the day for £3 a week, then working seven nights a week with the band for £35. It was pretty obvious which direction I should go, but the decision was made for me because I was fired from the shipyard for always falling asleep! So I turned pro at 17.

I carried on working in the North East, playing workingmen's clubs and nightclubs, but the band's music was becoming more progressive and the clubs didn't want that sort of thing. So at 21, I upped sticks and moved to London to seek my fortune.

I started off crashing on the floor of a friend in Shepherd's Bush, and I took a job on a building site to make ends meet. It was just me and about 200 Irishmen. Then I saw an advert for a 'wonder drummer' and my life changed. I rang the guy who'd placed the advert – Bryan Ferry. He recognised my accent, of course, and I think it helped that I was a Geordie like him. We had a rapport straight away.

When Roxy Music took off it was fantastic. For me, it was beyond successful. Coming from bands with a guitar and bass line-up, joining a band with a synthesiser and a sax player was really interesting. The glam look with the clothes and the make-up took me a while to get used to, being a jeans and baseball boots guy, but eventually I got the point of it. Before then, I'd never thought about 'making it' – I thought people who made it were something really special and, as a lad from Jarrow, I didn't see myself in that company. I feel I've been lucky. There are loads of great musicians who never get anywhere, but I had lots of enthusiasm and determination and was in the right place at the right time.

I stayed in London for 22 years, but all the time I was there I knew it was temporary – I was always going to move back to the North East which I did in 1994.

You appreciate the area more when you're older. I remember going to Hadrian's Wall as a kid and not thinking anything of it. Now it's one of my favourite places. There's a great spot near Haltwhistle called Cawfield Quarry where I used to go scuba-diving which is right by the wall. Everywhere you look there are fantastic views right along the wall – you can see for miles.

I've sort of gone back to my roots musically, having recently been playing for Ray Jackson's Lindisfarne. Apart from me, everyone else has been with the band at some stage so it's a real North East effort. I remember really clearly the first time I heard *Lady Eleanor* and I thought it was just remarkable. It's always a nice feeling when Geordies do well.

www.pauldrum.com

"There's a great spot near Haltwhistle called Cawfield Quarry where I used to go scuba-diving which is right by Hadrian's Wall. Everywhere you look there are fantastic views right along the wall – you can see for miles."

KATHRYN TICKELL

composer and performer

Kathryn Tickell, a virtuoso on the Northumbrian pipes and fiddle, has guested on five of superstar Sting's albums and is artistic director of the famous Sage Gateshead Folkworks programme. In 2009 she received the Queen's Medal for Music, awarded to artists judged to have made an exceptional contribution to British music, and in 2013 was awarded Musician of the Year at the BBC Radio 2 Folk awards for the second time in ten years.

I LOVE MY TYNE VALLEY HOME – it's an old mill house. We've been doing it up for several years now, but I think it will be a lifetime project. It's fantastic because it's exactly where my mum's family have been for hundreds of years and my dad's family have been here for a couple of generations.

Favourite Place – a track on my 2006 album *The Sky Didn't Fall* – is about my mum Kathleen's childhood growing up on Willowbog Farm in Warksburn in the 1940s and 1950s. She remembered the dances in a little place called Crookbank. It's a house now but in those days it was a school and my granddad was on the committee that organised the dances there. All the farmers and shepherds from the area would come along. It was a big social occasion and they took it all very seriously with tickets, and the women would put the supper out and serve tea from those big old-fashioned kettles.

My uncle Bill is just down the road and my dad is only about six miles away. When we first came to look at this house I suddenly recognised all the place names from the songs that my dad sings. I quoted all the songs to the people who lived here before us and they thought: "Yes, she should be living here."

It's always great to come back home. Even before I moved back to the countryside it always felt great to come back to the North East. From the ages of 18 to 23 I lived in Gateshead, before that we were in Tynemouth, then Newcastle. If I had been away on tour for a few weeks I used to love that feeling when you come back on the train and cross the Tyne. I still get that kick when I see the bridges. I actually grew up all over the place. We spent some of my childhood years in Lincolnshire and I remember my parents were always desperate to get back.

I think if people live away from home they tend to go on about getting back home much more than they would if they were actually there.

My dad Mike was always singing Northumberland songs and Border ballads. When I first started playing the piano all he wanted me to do was play *The Waters of Tyne*. It meant an awful lot to them, where they were from and that has had a big effect on me.

I'm sure things have changed a lot since my mother's day living in the Tyne Valley but there is still an amazing sense of community here.

I remember someone came to the house to deliver some wood and he knew all the Robson clan on

"I love this picture of Hareshaw Linn – linn is Scottish for waterfall – and I wrote a tune called Hareshaw Burn. I remember my granddad talking about it. On fine nights in the summer, when he and my granny were young, instead of having a dance in the village hall they would have an impromptu dance there. It's Arcadian and innocent. It looks like something out of Lord of the Rings. But it's still very much part of village life – kids from the village still go there for the annual Easter egg hunt."

The Kathryn Tickell Band

Kathryn rehearsing with Sting at the Sage Gateshead

my mother's side. He went through the entire family. Then I found I could remember bits about his family. My grandparents would be constantly talking about who was related to who. It was part of growing up and who you were. Some people might find it a bit intrusive, but I love it. It makes you feel you belong.

When we moved here I asked the people for the front door key and they looked completely blank. They hadn't locked the door for 18 years and couldn't actually find the key. So for the first year we lived here every time we went out the house was completely open! It's all secure now because we have just had a new front door put on. But that's a mark of how safe it is around here.

I've always been a big fan of Sting – it was great playing on his albums after being into The Police as a teenager – and musicians like Northumbrian folk legend Alistair Anderson who was in the original line-up of the High Level Ranters from 1968-1979.

It was very unusual to actually make a living out of traditional folk music at that time and Alistair was out there doing it. He's incredibly generous of spirit; a lot of people might have seen me as competition coming up, but it never appeared to cross his mind.

I'm still finding out things that he did for me that I didn't know at the time. People say I remember when we first booked you in 1986 and we did because Alistair said we should. He was singing my praises and helping me like he helped so many others.

He's a visionary. Without him we wouldn't have Folkworks – the Sage Gateshead's acclaimed folk music development agency for the North East – and we wouldn't have the folk music degree at Newcastle University.

I was also incredibly lucky to get to meet a lot of the older generation of traditional musicians; people like Will Atkinson who played the mouth organ – or 'moothie' as he called it – fiddle players Willie Taylor and Dick Moscrop and piper Joe Hutton. I spent a lot of time with them when I was little and learned a lot of tunes from them.

They were my friends and are sadly missed. But in a way they are still there for me – whenever I play a Willie Taylor tune I can still hear him playing it along with me inside my head. That's a wonderful thing about music – that people can live on through their tunes.

www.kathryntickell.com

"Alistair Anderson is a visionary. Without him we wouldn't have Folkworks – the Sage Gateshead's acclaimed folk music development agency for the North East."

STEPHEN TOMPKINSON

actor

Teessider Stephen Tompkinson is one of the most in-demand actors on TV, best known for his work in dramas including DCI Banks, Wild at Heart, Ballykissangel *and* Grafters.

I HAVE VERY FOND MEMORIES of growing up in Stockton, endless summers playing down at the Rec and being taken to Ayresome Park, which is where Mam and Dad did their courting. It's still very much a part of me and very dear to my heart. It feels like coming home. Every holiday was spent in Stockton-on-Tees with the family. I was about six when I first saw 'Boro play. It was Jack Charlton's aces in those days. I remember coming home and saying: "Mam, I spoke to Jack Charlton and I got a silk scarf from him." I still have it. I've been a Middlesbrough supporter all my life and I do my best to see 'Boro when I can. Everyone admires Steve Gibson. He's one of the most honest and faithful chairmen in the game – and long may he continue.

We are a very close family. Before Mam and Dad got married, Dad's eldest brother married Mam's eldest sister. I had an aunt and uncle who lived in Windermere Road in Stockton and my grandma and granddad lived further down the same road and opposite them in Grangefield Road was my dad's brother and Mam's sister.

My first memory of television was watching Laurel and Hardy with my granddad. Everyone else was laughing at Ollie. My granddad sat me on his knee and said "watch Stan." To me it seemed like he was doing nothing but Granddad could see his genius. That's what made me want to become an actor.

A lot of my family are still in Stockton but Auntie Eileen and Uncle Bernard moved to Whitley Bay. We spent Christmas with them a few years ago for their 40th wedding anniversary. We all went to Tynemouth beach and braved the elements. It was packed. It's a gorgeous beach and it was great to see it so full of families with people walking their dogs.

"I was about six when I first saw 'Boro play. It was Jack Charlton's aces in those days."

Tynemouth beach is one of my favourite views, especially from one of the bedrooms at the Grand Hotel. I'm a huge fan of Stan and Ollie so that's a favourite place of mine because they stayed there and the place always gives me a warm feeling. But I've always adored the whole North East coast. It's so rugged it just blows all the cobwebs away.

I had a ball when I filmed *Grafters* in the North East with Robson Green. I got all the family along to Whitley Bay when we did it. Robson and I were friends before but it was great to get the opportunity to go to work together every day. We still keep in touch.

"I love the Grand Hotel. I'm a huge fan of Stan and Ollie so that's a favourite place of mine because they stayed there and the place always gives me a warm feeling."

BECKY UNTHANK

singer and musician

The Unthanks – Rachel Unthank and younger sister Becky – are known for their eclectic approach in combining traditional English folk music with other musical genres. They won the Horizon category at the 2008 BBC Radio 2 Folk Awards.

AS KIDS GROWING UP IN RYTON we were lucky to have the Willows on our doorstep. At the bottom of the steep bank we ran around the meadow that led to the River Tyne. There are a number of hollows on the grassland to prevent enemy planes landing in the Second World War – particularly fun to run up and down with our dog Bonny. Either side of the bank were woods with tall trees where we'd pick conkers in the autumn and collect holly in the winter to decorate the house. There was also a pond, a home to swans in the summer. My mam actually walked across this frozen pond when she was eight months pregnant with me!

We would go to folk festivals each summer. We were surrounded by music and loved it. We saw people like Norma Waterson who was a big inspiration as well as acts like the French Canadian band La Bottine Souriante. My dad was in The Keelers, an unaccompanied harmony group, and we'd also hear North East singers like Johnny Handle and The Wilsons. Mam and Dad would teach us songs all the way in the car to and from the festivals. Rachel and I clog-danced in Addison Rapper and Clog Team (named after the pit in Ryton where we grew up). Our dad was part of the rapper team so we'd get free tickets to the festivals. Later when we were no longer dancing with the team we had to think of new ways of getting there. So Rachel and I decided to try to convince organisers to let us come and sing for a ticket. That's how our career started!

Folkworks is a brilliant organisation for folk artists growing up in the North East. They did, and still do, run workshop days and weekends. It brought to our attention not only local artists but interesting collaborations such as SWAP, a Swedish/English band. As a teenager me and my best friend would venture into Newcastle to the student unions, bars, nightclubs and jazz clubs – anywhere we could get in as 15-year-olds disguised as students. We heard jazz, pop, indie, hip hop, funk, ska and we were into it all. Although my first record was probably something like Boyzone, bought at the Metro Centre, I quickly moved onto quirky indie stuff like Belle and Sebastian.

The North East has some great performance spaces. We performed in the round, in the Great Hall at the Discovery Museum in Newcastle a few years ago, and it felt like a really special gig. Having the Sage on our side of the river is fantastic and something we're very proud of too. I fondly remember an early Rachel Unthank and the Winterset gig upstairs in the Cumberland Arms in the Ouseburn Valley. It's such a folky hub at the Cumberland with rapper teams practising there, music sessions and gigs – you'll always bump into people you know there.

The Tyneside Cinema is a great independent art deco cinema where *Songs from the Shipyards* was created and first performed – a new experience in terms of performance space. Sunderland Minster has recently started putting on gigs, and we also performed the Shipyards film there. It was a stunning setting. Those great characters still make me laugh, and the line "Let Swan Hunter's epitaph be: Being best wasn't good enough" still makes me cry.

The people of the North East are known for being friendly, down-to-earth and warm with a certain amount of directness. I am lucky to have many places to call home in the North East. My dad still lives in Ryton. We record and rehearse a lot where my sister and husband Adrian live next to a farm in beautiful Northumberland. My mam's at the coast in Cullercoats so I love the beaches, Tynemouth market and 'happy hour' pizza on the fish quay! As a fan of Turner's paintings, Dunstanburgh has always struck me as a special place – there is something about the light there. No wonder Turner loved to paint it so much. In Newcastle, one of my favourite things to do is walk from Grey's Monument, down past all those grand buildings to the Quayside, or along to Ouseburn Valley or to the Free Trade pub where you can have a pint and take in the view of our magnificent river and its bridges.

www.the-unthanks.com

"In Newcastle, one of my favourite things to do is walk from Grey's Monument, down past all those grand buildings to the Quayside."

"We were lucky to have the Willows on our doorstep. At the bottom of the steep bank we ran around the meadow that led to the River Tyne."

MENS
OUTFITTING
The
Litewear
The
Newcastle
Latest.
CASH'S

RACHEL UNTHANK

singer and musician

The Unthanks – Rachel Unthank and younger sister Becky – are known for their eclectic approach in combining traditional English folk music with other musical genres. They won the Horizon category at the 2008 BBC Radio 2 Folk Awards.

OUR MAM AND DAD were huge influences on us musically. They both love folk music and took us to loads of festivals where we were exposed to concerts, ceilidhs and song and music sessions. One of my fondest earliest memories is of sitting under a table at a sing-around with my sticker book, soaking up all the wonderful stories that these adults were singing to each other. It was like being allowed into a secret magical world of musical stories.

As kids we went to see loads of folk concerts which were always exciting – especially those organised by Folkworks at the Sage Gateshead. I remember sitting in Saltwell Park on a balmy summer evening for one such performance. Some of the first concerts I went to myself as a teenager were from slightly different genres. I remember going to see Bryan Adams at Gateshead Stadium when I was 14. Me and my friends felt really grown up even though our parents picked us up afterwards. I also queued from 11am on a freezing November morning to see Extreme at Whitley Bay Ice Rink, which definitely felt like a rite of passage. But I am afraid to say that the first record that I ever bought was New Kids on the Block's single *The Right Stuff* from HMV in Newcastle.

Performing in the North East is always special. Playing with the Brighouse and Rastrick Brass Band in Durham Cathedral four weeks after our first child arrived will be a privilege I remember forever. You feel the warmth of the audience, and there are always friends and family there to share the moment with you. I think it's tough to describe the qualities of people from the North East when you are one of those people yourself. But I enjoy the region's sense of fun and admire its survival instinct. I also think we're a welcoming region, which is maybe explained by how our communities have been enriched and diversified over the centuries by people from all over the world who arrived here from across the seas.

I now live near Corbridge in the Tyne Valley and I love the view out on to the fields and gently rolling hills, with the trees always marking the change of the seasons. After a hectic tour it feels like a secret place to escape back to. Northumberland has a charged atmosphere – it can be eerie to look at the peaceful, open landscape and remember it was once a bloody and lawless place. It can be both beautiful and bleakly stark. Northumberland is an endlessly fascinating and complex place.

One of my favourite views in the world is when you walk down the hill towards Newton-by-the Sea and the coastal sweep opens up before you, with Dunstanburgh Castle on the horizon. It doesn't matter what the weather is, the sight always makes me feel so glad. A very special place. We hold singing weekends up near there in North Sunderland, near Seahouses, where people come from all over the place to spend a winter weekend with us. We sing, eat good food, drink good beer, walk and sing on the beach, have a lively singing session in a cosy local pub, then go back to Springhill Farm bunkhouse and sing some more. I think people are drawn here because of the dramatic backdrop of the scenery. They really feel like they have come on an adventure.

I never met Sir Bobby Robson, but his passion, warmth and humanity make you feel proud that he represented this region. We're told that he liked our music, and it's a thrill to think he even heard it. It was a real honour to be part of the celebration concert at the Sage Gateshead in 2013 and we were very humbled to be asked and proud to be able to offer a small part towards the celebration of such a universally-loved man.

The Tyneside Cinema brought us together with film-maker Richard Fenwick to collaborate on a film called *Songs from the Shipyards*, with a live soundtrack, about the shipbuilding industry. We really wanted to tell a story, and to celebrate the industry without falling into sentimentality. It's a fine line to tread, showing the respect we have for the people who worked hard – without glorifying their lives – as honest, decent, proper people. They were great days, but it's important to remember that they were tough and dangerous days too. Whilst researching this project I discovered that older generations of our family, who are predominantly from Teesside, worked on the docks on the Tees. But *Songs from the Shipyards* is likely to affect anyone with connections to an area in which industry was once the lifeblood of the community. The film could be seen as an illustration of Britain's industrial journey in microcosm, and could just as easily be about the mills or the mines.

www.the-unthanks.com

"One of my favourite views in the world is when you walk down the hill towards Newton-by-the Sea and the coastal sweep opens up before you, with Dunstanburgh Castle on the horizon."

SID WADDELL 1940-2012

TV sports commentator and writer

© Ross Parry Picture Agency

Sid Waddell – the 'voice of darts' – was famous for his wild, ranting Sky TV commentaries. He was awarded Sports Commentator of the Year in 2002 and wrote 11 books, including biographies of darts players.

MY FATHER BOB got up every day and crawled out under the North Sea working as a coalface drawer – which meant he was jammed in a claustrophobic tunnel pulling the roof down as he went and hoping it wouldn't collapse on him and kill him.

The highest wage he put on the table was £11 and 10 shillings for 48 years down Ellington Colliery and when he retired they mis-spelled his name on a commemorative scroll, calling him Weddell.

He had angina by the time I went to Cambridge so he had to go on lighter work and was putting about £9 and 10 shillings on the table in 1958. So my mother Martha got a job scrubbing floors at the workingmen's club for £2 a week.

Without a big supportive family of workers and savers I would probably have ended up selling fruit at Ashington market.

The shadow of the pit dominated my childhood and everybody in the village of Lynemouth, which had a population of about 3,000. There were 700 men working down the pit at Lynemouth or Ellington Colliery and we knew there would be an average of four deaths every year. We lived in constant fear of horrific injuries. We knew Auld Betty (the pitmen's nickname for the colliery, named after a daughter of coal baron Francis Priestman) is going to take your thumb, your eye, give you angina or kill you. There was massive respect for birth, marriage, death and family.

My father used to sit and guard his leek trench at night with a shotgun. It wasn't loaded but he took that much pride in his vegetable garden.

© Beamish Museum

A miner setting his props at the coalface

I remember the sanctity of life there. I was brought up with respect for what my father did and how that gives the village butcher a living and how it puts money behind the till at the workingmen's club. There was self-policing and if you misbehaved the copper would slap you around the ear. Employment was the key to happiness.

My parents had no idea where they were sending me when I went to Cambridge. My mother was Catholic and religious. She wanted me to be a priest and my father wanted me to be a maths scholar and become a nuclear scientist. But the highest I ever got in maths was fourth in the class. I was good at history and finished with a very good 2:1 degree in Modern History.

I had a photographic memory. I remember at school I memorised the entire Penguin History of Europe 1850-1914 and if you said: "What's on page 33?" I could tell you.

But the fear of my father dying in the pit was why I kept up a façade of religiousness as a kid. From the age of eight I went to Alnwick Convent. When I passed the 11-plus at Ellington Primary School my granny wanted me to go to the Catholic grammar school in Newcastle, St Cuthbert's. But Bob said: "I'm not having Sidney getting

"My favourite view has to be Alnwick Castle. I once scored both goals in the annual Shrove Tuesday football match played in the shadow of Alnwick Castle. It was in 1956 when I was 16 years old."

Sid, far right, celebrating his Cambridge scholarship with his mates in the Joiners Arms in Morpeth, Christmas 1958

up at 6am to come back 12 hours later just for religion." So I went to Morpeth Grammar.

They were both very funny people too, great sense of humour. My dad was Scottish and my mother was of Irish extraction. After I left Cambridge I had no bloody idea what I wanted to do. My first job was as a cost clerk at Ashington Colliery for £7 a week. In 1964 I wrote a play, which won a national prize from the BBC, and I went to London as their guest. I met The Animals who were there to do *Top of the Pops* but were more busy chatting up the sexy dancers in Pan's People.

I wore grey flannels and a hacking jacket and looked a complete geek but I got on with them and Eric Burdon asked me to be their road manager for the night!

After the show we went to a Soho pub and suddenly I'm drinking pints with Paul Jones and Manfred Mann, and Chris Farlowe and Zoot Money who had all been on the show. It was unreal.

My favourite view has to be Alnwick Castle. I once scored both goals in the annual Shrove Tuesday football match played in the shadow of Alnwick Castle. It was in 1956 when I was 16 years old and played for St Michael's parish. I was carried off shoulder-high and got 15 bob for each goal so I went on the beer with my uncle Sam to celebrate at my favourite pub, The Joiners Arms in Morpeth – the best boozer in the world. I went back to school two days later and told them I had been off with asthma. But unfortunately my picture was all over the front page of the Northumberland Gazette.

Here are ten of our favourite memorable one-liners to savour from Sid's glittering 30-year career as a darts commentator with the BBC and Sky.

- If Cliff gets back in this it will be the greatest comeback since Lazarus
- It's the kind of jousting we used to see when Ivanhoe was stuffing the Normans
- Bristow reasons; Bristow quickens; aahhh, Bristow!
- He looks about as happy as a penguin in a microwave
- This lad has more checkouts than Tesco's
- We couldn't have more excitement if Elvis walked in and asked for a chip sandwich
- It's the nearest thing to a public execution you'll see this side of Saudi Arabia
- If we'd had Taylor at Hastings, the Normans would have turned around and gone home
- We've got a ding dong verily on Sky
- Four legs on the trot – this is Strictly Come Darting

"I went on the beer with my uncle Sam to celebrate at my favourite pub, The Joiners Arms in Morpeth – the best boozer in the world."

FRANCIS WATSON-ARMSTRONG

farmer and keeper of Bamburgh Castle

Francis Watson-Armstrong describes himself as the 'present-day keeper' of one of the country's most iconic landmarks – Bamburgh Castle – which has been his family seat since 1894. His aim is to conserve and enhance the castle for future generations of his family and for the public. He also runs a farm in Bamburgh.

IN MY HEART I'M A NORTHUMBRIAN, even though I was born in London and went to school there. My family owned Bamburgh Castle and, until 1970 when the National Trust took it over, Cragside in Rothbury. We used to go to Northumberland for our holidays and I always felt more comfortable there than anywhere else. It's always been my stomping ground. Now I live on the farm I run just outside Bamburgh and I walk on the beach by the castle with my dogs every morning and I think how lucky I am.

Talking of luck, I won the lottery in life because I was given up as a baby and adopted by my parents who brought me to this wonderful part of the world. I remember as a child going to Cragside and finding it amazing but very spooky to stay there at nights. Bamburgh Castle could feel haunted as well, but it was great fun. Wherever we went, there were interesting people around. I remember my father playing backgammon with the Duke of Northumberland, drinking whisky and telling choice stories. I took over the estate in 1987 when my father died, I've been here ever since and I'll be in this area for good. I may own Bamburgh Castle, along with my sister, but I don't think of myself as owner – I feel more like the keeper of the place for my three children, the next generation.

I was a bit of a wild child, I suppose. I remember joyriding round Seahouses in my father's Rolls-Royce when I was 13 or 14 with my head just poking above the steering wheel – I hope he never knew – and I still love driving, both cars and motor bikes. I'm a total petrol-head and one of my great pleasures in life is haring round the Northumberland hills with AC/DC on at full volume.

"I remember as a child going to Cragside and finding it amazing but very spooky to stay there at nights."

That was the band that I loved best as a lad, and that has stayed with me. I've got all their albums and the singer Brian Johnson, a Geordie, is an absolute hero of mine.

My other hero is my ancestor, the first Lord Armstrong. He was a pioneering inventor and engineer who developed Cragside and restored Bamburgh Castle. A very impressive man.

The castle is a labour of love for me, and one that never ends. It's like painting the Forth Bridge – as soon as you think you've finished what needs doing you have to start again. But I have a great team running it. The castle is open to the public, attracting over 100,000 visitors a year. Its unique make-up and views make it popular as a wedding venue too. It's many people's favourite place in the North, not just mine.

www.bamburghcastle.com

"I walk on the beach by the castle with my dogs every morning and I think how lucky I am."

DENISE WELCH

actress, dancer and television presenter

Denise acted alongside fellow North Easterners in Byker Grove, Auf Wiedersehen, Pet *and* Spender. *She is best known for her roles in* Coronation Street *and* Waterloo Road *and for presenting* Loose Women. *She was a contestant in* Dancing on Ice *in 2011 and won* Celebrity Big Brother *in 2012. She and former husband Tim Healy have two sons.*

I'M A FULLY PAID-UP MEMBER of the Geordie Mafia. I live in Cheshire but I keep in touch with my mates from the North East and we still look out for each other. Jill Halfpenny is a friend, Ian La Frenais is my godfather and of course I still see a lot of Tim, even though we're not married any more. We got divorced Geordie-style – we're great pals and we always will be.

A lot of people almost apologise for where they're from as if they were ashamed of it, but we're proud of our roots. I think it's something special about the Geordie character. People are so pleased for you if you have a bit of success and genuinely sorry when things go wrong. Everybody supports what you do. The people I know have celebrated every single thing I have done, and the newspapers and TV in the region have done the same. They don't try to knock you down.

Wherever I may live, the North East will always be home. I've recently revisited some of the places where I grew up and it was quite an emotional journey. My first home was in Monkseaton, but we moved when I was a baby to Cullercoats to my nana and grandpa's house in Beverley Terrace. My parents were only 21 and they were the youngest of their gang to have children, but they just carried on with their lives as normal, always having parties with their friends around. The 'party animal' side of me clearly started there!

Later we moved to Monkseaton and my dad Vin was cajoled into joining Welch's Toffees – the family business. It probably didn't really suit him, but my grandpa was a bit of a disciplinarian and insisted on it. My dad had been to university and studied economics but he

Slack Lasses: Andrea McLean and Denise in Sunday for Sammy in a spoof of ITV's Loose Women

was a performer by nature. He did lots of amateur dramatics at that time and he did turn pro many years later. Even now he still does his party piece as a drag queen called Raquel.

But the toffee business was a big part of all our lives. Strangely I never had a sweet tooth as a child but I used to love going to the factory to watch the blackcurrant lollies coming out of the oven, and my sister Debbie and I would be very popular when we took friends there. They even called me Truly Scrumptious. My grandfather invented Black Bullets and today the smell of them is so evocative of my childhood: it takes me straight back.

We had a freedom in those days that I'd never allow my son Louis. My mum would wave Debbie and I off for junior school, both of us wearing fluorescent flashes, when I was only about eight. When I was 11 they sent me to La Sagesse in Jesmond. I'd get the bus on my own to Newcastle then cross the road to Marlborough Crescent and get another bus out to Jesmond.

When I was 12 the family business went down and we moved to Ebchester in County Durham to a little white cottage which looked to me like something out of Hansel and Gretel. I loved it and my dad still lives there. Around that time I left La Sagesse and went to Consett Grammar where I was much happier.

I got into acting at school, then at 18 I went off to drama school in London. I was lucky that a lot of work came my way both on stage and on TV, so I stayed

"The view from the beach up to Tynemouth Priory is one I still love to this day."

"Tim and I were incredibly flattered and very honoured to receive the joint Silver Heart."

Interior of the Live Theatre

mostly in London, although I did a lot of work at the Live Theatre in Newcastle where I cut my teeth in the acting world. It was a great place for new actors and writers. Tom Hadaway was a brilliant local writer who never received the national acclaim he deserved. He was a great inspiration for me.

It wasn't until I had my first son Matthew when I was 30 that I got this strong homing instinct and just felt I had to move back to the North East. Tim was all for it, so we bought a lovely home in High Mickley and moved there. It has incomparable views over the Tyne Valley and it's still one of my favourite views ever.

Then the *Coronation Street* job came along and we moved to the North West, thinking we'd just be there a few months but it ended up with us staying there, as it was so much easier for work.

But I still come home a lot, and I still have the same feeling about the area. As well as the Tyne Valley, I always love going back to Whitley Bay and Tynemouth. I would have loved to take my son Louis to the Spanish City which has a place in a lot of people's hearts. And Tim's in Whitley Bay always had the best fish and chips ever. I also remember when I was a child – before anyone knew about the problems the sun could cause the skin – my mum sunbathing on Tynemouth beach. We'd go there for picnics and she would smear herself with olive oil, take a kitchen clock timer and turn over every 30 minutes. The view from the beach up to Tynemouth Priory is one I still love to this day.

I think one of the things I'm proudest of – apart from my children, of course – is the fact I've been able to get involved with charities and good causes in the region such as Children North East, Mind and Sunday for Sammy. Tim and I were incredibly flattered and very honoured to receive the joint Silver Heart award from the Variety Club at Newcastle Civic Centre in 2009 in recognition of the work we do for charity. It's their highest honour and it's the first time in the charity's 60-year history that a joint Silver Heart has been awarded. It's always great to be appreciated by your own in your home area.

I don't want to come over as Saint Denise of Whitley Bay – it's just that the North East has given a lot to me and my family and I'm glad that now I can give something back to the North East.

www.officialdenisewelch.co.uk

"Live Theatre in Newcastle is a great place for new actors and writers to cut their teeth." A view across the Newcastle rooftops from the Live Theatre

KEVIN WHATELY

actor

Actor Kevin Whately, from Humshaugh, Northumberland is best known for his role as Robert 'Robbie' Lewis in the ITV crime dramas Lewis *and* Inspector Morse *and his role as hen-pecked Geordie brickie Neville Hope in the ITV comedy drama* Auf Wiedersehen, Pet. *He lives in Bedfordshire with actress wife Madelaine Newton.*

I GREW UP IN THE TYNE VALLEY where we were surrounded by fields. There was a dairy farm nearby and one of my earliest memories was helping with the milking as a little boy. We lived less than half a mile from the River Tyne so I would spend many happy hours down there walking with our dog – a collie/Labrador cross – where there was a huge sandbank laid down by the river. It was a great place for kids to play.

I went to Humshaugh First School – there were four classes and you left at 14. You would have three years worth of pupils in each class, so five to seven-year-olds would all sit together but doing different school work. Most of my classmates seemed to end up as garage mechanics. I'm still in touch with some of my school chums but like me they are coming up to retirement age now! One or two of us passed the 11-plus and I was lucky enough to go to Barnard Castle School. There was a local businessman called Mungo Campbell who set up an educational trust in memory of his wife, and it paid for my brother and I to go there. I was a boarder. I hated it at first but a school like that provided a lot of opportunity, and by the time I reached the sixth form I was well into drama and doing plays at school – so that was my introduction to acting.

Kevin as Inspector Robbie Lewis with DS Hathaway, played by Laurence Fox, in the ITV drama Lewis

A special view for me is the vista from Heavenfield, at the top of Brunton Bank. St Oswald's church is there – built on the burial site of Oswald, king of Northumbria who defeated the Welsh in the Battle of Heavenfield in 634. It's especially poignant for me because my parents are buried there. My sister was married there too.

It's on the road east of Chollerford that runs alongside the Roman wall and a stone cross marks the site of the Battle of Heavenfield. It's a beautiful little place. The church doesn't even have electricity so they only have one service a month and it has a foot-pumped harmonium.

My favourite view on the Northumberland coast has to be from the 15th tee on Bamburgh golf course. It's an absolutely stunning panorama. You can see for miles and miles in different directions. You can look back inland to the Cheviots and over to Bamburgh Castle or out to the Farne Islands and beyond to Lindisfarne Castle.

We always used to go up to the Northumberland coast for summer family holidays when I was growing up. It was actually within striking distance for day trips from where we lived but in the summer we would

"A special view for me is the vista from Heavenfield."

"Heavenfield is especially poignant for me because my parents are buried there in the graveyard at St Oswald's church."

normally rent a cottage for the holidays. There would be about 10 or 12 of us including cousins, aunts and uncles. My mother did it in her day and we have done it with our kids and now even with our granddaughter. It's a family tradition.

A big part of me would love to go back and live in the North East. I've been away for 40 years now but I still miss the people. I miss the weather up there too. The winters always seemed hard in the Fifties and Sixties. I remember cross-country running in it. I wanted to be Jim Alder or Brendan Foster and I was always slipping around in the snow and mud, up to my oxters in it. Snow and cold, and no central heating but I loved it and still do. I would love to live up in Northumberland again.

I also feel privileged to be part of the biennial Sunday for Sammy concerts at Newcastle City Hall. I remember seeing all my heroes there like The Who and Led Zeppelin and to be on stage and feel all that warmth from the audience in your home city is an amazing feeling. It's great just to sit in it, never mind play it. The venue is astonishing.

"My favourite view of the North East coast has to be from the 15th tee on Bamburgh golf course."

INDEX OF PLACES

"EVERY DAY I SEE THE ANGEL
AND IT REMINDS ME THAT I'M HOME."
SIR BOBBY ROBSON 1933-2009